Abstract Thinking – A 30-Day Mindset Transformation Guide

Daily Lessons for Consuming and Translating Abstract Concepts into Actionable Meaning

Part of the *30-Day Mindset Transformation Series*

Other Books in the 30-Day Mindset Transformation Series

Reliability – A 30-Day Mindset Transformation Guide

Daily Lessons in Evidence-Based Thinking to Create a Reliability Mindset

---

Change & Culture – A 30-Day Mindset Transformation Guide

Daily Lessons Using the R3/R4 Change Model™ to Create a Shift in the Culture of Your Organization

---

Safety & Risk – A 30-Day Mindset Transformation Guide

Daily Lessons In Evidence-Based Safety: Merging Human Leadership and System Discipline

---

Problem-Solving – A 30-Day Mindset Transformation Guide

Daily Lessons in How to See Problems Differently and Develop More Effective Solutions

---

Communications – A 30-Day Mindset Transformation Guide

Daily Lessons to Reframe Communication as a Leadership Discipline, Not a Soft Skill

---

Sustainable Performance – A 30-Day Mindset Transformation Guide

Daily Lessons to Engineer Consistency, Prevent Burnout, and Sustain Results That Matter

Abstract Thinking – A 30-Day Mindset Transformation Guide

Daily Lessons for Consuming and Translating Abstract Concepts into Actionable Meaning

Andy Page, Ph.D.

Published by EBR Technologies

ISBN: 979-8-9941269-2-9

Printed in the United States of America
Published by EBR Technologies

Disclaimer

This book is intended for educational and professional development purposes. The concepts, methods, and examples presented reflect the author's experience and interpretation of best practices within the fields of maintenance, reliability, and organizational culture.

While every effort has been made to ensure accuracy and clarity, the information provided is not a substitute for sound engineering judgment, professional advice, or site-specific analysis. Readers are encouraged to adapt these ideas to their own organizations responsibly, with appropriate technical validation and safety consideration.

Neither the author nor EBR Technologies, LLC assumes any responsibility for outcomes resulting from the application of the material in this book. All implementation decisions remain the sole responsibility of the reader and their organization.

Names and examples of companies, individuals, and situations have been used for illustrative purposes only and do not represent actual entities or events unless explicitly stated.

Table of Contents

Bonus Materials

Dedication

For the people who refuse to accept fog as fate,
who sense there is structure beneath the surface
and are determined to find it.

For the ones who slow down long enough to think,
to question what others rush past,
and to search for the mechanism instead of the noise.

For the leaders who translate complexity into clarity,
who build understanding in others,
and who treat ideas with the same discipline they bring to action.

For the learners who stay curious,
who take comfort in the work of thinking,
and who know that intelligence grows when you give it form.

For the individuals who believe meaning can be made,
patterns can be recognized,
and insight can be engineered.

This book is for everyone committed to building the architecture of their own mind,
to strengthening the structures that shape clarity,
and to becoming a person who understands deeply—
and helps others understand as well.

Abstract

Abstract thinking is not an innate talent or a mark of intellectual giftedness—it is a system of mental practices that make complex ideas feel coherent, navigable, and usable. This book challenges the belief that understanding is a mysterious spark or a trait some people naturally possess, and instead shows that clarity emerges from structure, mechanism, pattern recognition, and disciplined interpretation. Across thirty days, readers learn to build the cognitive architecture that allows them to absorb ideas more deeply, separate signal from noise, and translate complexity into meaning they can act on.

The framework introduced here redefines understanding as a process that can be engineered, strengthened, and transferred across domains. Through deliberate slowing, layered analysis, mechanism-first thinking, and intentional reconstruction, individuals learn to shift from passive consumption to active comprehension. The book emphasizes that real understanding requires seeing beyond surface information—identifying invisible forces, interrogating assumptions, detecting recurring patterns, and articulating governing principles—while also cultivating the ability to explain ideas cleanly and help others see what they cannot yet perceive.

By integrating cognitive science, mental modeling, systems thinking, and applied learning strategies, this guide provides a practical pathway for anyone seeking clarity that endures beyond the moment. Abstract thinking becomes less about being "smart" and more about using a repeatable method to make complex ideas simple, stable, and transferable. The result is a disciplined approach to understanding—one that expands capability, sharpens judgment, and elevates how people think, learn, and lead.

Author's Note

Bringing order to chaos is a real-life human superpower. Not the comic-book kind, but the quiet ability to walk into a swirl of information, emotion, assumptions, and noise—and pull out something coherent. Something usable. Something true. I've always been drawn to that moment when confusion gives way to clarity, when the mind snaps into alignment and suddenly the world makes more sense than it did a minute earlier. It feels less like discovering an answer and more like uncovering the structure that was there all along.

I never thought this ability was instinct, reserved for people wired a certain way. I always believed that people can actually just think, and that the pattern oftentimes reveals itself and becomes impossible to ignore. Real thinkers don't rely on talent. They rely on frameworks—ways of grouping ideas, probing mechanisms, noticing invisible forces, naming principles, and stripping away noise until only the structure remained. The clarity looks effortless, but the method underneath it was anything but accidental.

This book comes from watching how thinkers think. It's an attempt to—outline the scaffolding, the layers, the mechanisms, the patterns, the principles, and the translation tools that make clarity a repeatable outcome rather than a lucky break. Across these pages, my aim isn't to tell you what to think but to show you how to build the internal system that allows you to think with precision, depth, and confidence.

If one idea stays with you after reading, let it be this:
the mind is not a container for information—it is an instrument.
And when you tune the instrument, clarity becomes something you can create on demand.

— Andy Page, Ph.D.
Founder, EBR Technologies

Foreword

In every field—from business to education to engineering to everyday life—people are surrounded by more information than any generation before them. Yet despite this abundance, one pattern appears again and again: individuals move through complex situations without a reliable way to make sense of what they encounter. They gather data, collect opinions, react to pressures, and try to keep pace with constant change, but without a structure for thinking, clarity becomes unpredictable and understanding becomes fragile.

Most people don't struggle because ideas are too difficult. They struggle because they approach abstraction the same way they approach urgent tasks—by leaning on speed, memory, or intuition. But intuition doesn't reveal mechanisms. Memory doesn't organize meaning. Speed doesn't separate signal from noise. Without an underlying architecture, thinking becomes crowded, effortful, and inconsistent, no matter how capable or intelligent the person may be.

Across organizations, classrooms, families, and teams, the same themes surface. People want clarity but operate without design. They want insight but rely on familiarity. They want good decisions but lack the structure that makes those decisions reproducible. They want alignment but communicate conclusions instead of underlying principles. The result is often overwhelm, drift, misunderstanding, and a persistent sense that thinking should feel easier than it does.

The challenge is not a lack of intelligence—it is a lack of method. Human beings are rarely taught how to handle abstraction, how to hold complexity still long enough to examine it, or how to move from scattered details to organized meaning. Most people enter adulthood with highly developed technical or interpersonal skills, yet without the mental models that turn information into insight. As the demands of modern life accelerate, this gap becomes even more visible: conversations become more reactive, decisions more emotional, and collaboration more difficult, not because people refuse to understand, but because they lack a framework that allows understanding to take shape.

5

Abstract thinking offers a different path. When ideas are sorted into buckets, when mechanisms are identified, when patterns are recognized, when principles are named, when layers are distinguished, and when meaning is compressed into its usable form, thinking becomes a process rather than a struggle. Understanding becomes something that can be built, strengthened, and transferred—not a moment of inspiration, but a repeatable practice. The fog lifts not because the mind tries harder, but because the mind has a system to follow.

A structured thinker becomes more than someone who understands. They become someone who stabilizes the environment around them. They reduce confusion in conversations. They clarify direction in teams. They help others see what they previously overlooked. They translate complexity into meaning and meaning into action. Over time, their presence elevates the collective intelligence of the people they work with. This is the practical power of conceptual skill—its effects compound outward.

The world consistently rewards people who can understand deeply, think structurally, and communicate clearly.
- Teams depend on them.
- Leaders rely on them.
- Decisions improve because of them.
- Cultures strengthen around them.
- Understanding is not a gift—it is an architecture.
- A pattern that can be learned, refined, and expanded over time.

The hope is that this book helps readers build that architecture with intention, so that clarity becomes a capability they can trust—not just when conditions are calm, but especially when they are not.

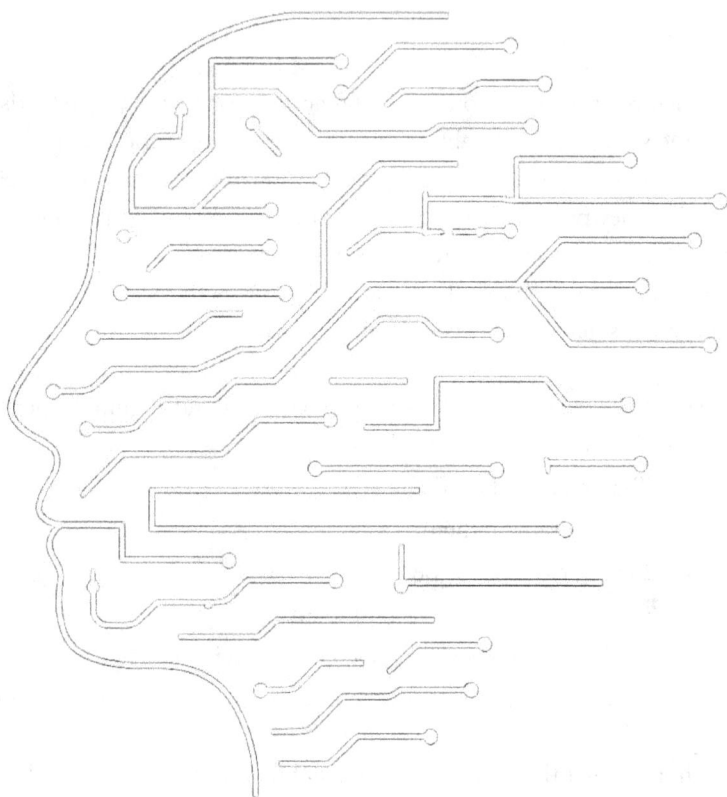

How to Use This 30-Day Guide

This book is designed to be worked through, not skimmed.
Each day introduces a single shift in how you understand, organize, or translate ideas. Not vague inspiration. Not intellectual decoration. A targeted upgrade you can apply immediately to the way you process information, solve problems, or make sense of the world. The aim is simple: refine your thinking a little each day until clarity becomes instinctive.

Don't layer these entries on top of multitasking.
Approach them with a quiet mind. Read one day, pause, and give the idea room to take shape. The real value isn't in the paragraph—it's in the practice. Abstract thinking improves through repetition: slow passes, clear steps, and deliberate structure. The more you use the tools, the more automatic they become.

Each entry follows a consistent rhythm:

- **The Lesson** — A shift in how to see, structure, or interpret complex ideas.
- **The Reflection** — A focused prompt that helps you examine the patterns shaping your understanding.
- **The Commitment** — A small, intentional action that strengthens the architecture of your thinking.
- **The EBR Principle** — A distilled truth that anchors the day's concept in a broader pattern.

Treat the book as a 30-day rebuild of your cognitive operating system.
You are not collecting clever ideas—you are constructing mental architecture. Move through the days steadily. Reread when needed. Apply each shift in real situations.

By the end, you won't just understand abstract thinking—
you'll be using it to bring order to complexity wherever you find it.

Why the Emphasis on Mindsets?

Every improvement journey begins with a decision — and every decision begins with a mindset. Before you can change what people do, you have to change what they believe about what matters. That's why every book in this series starts with thinking, not tools. Procedures and policies don't stick if the people inside the system still see the world the same way.

Mindset is the hidden architecture of behavior — the lens through which we interpret data, make judgments, and justify choices. When the frame is wrong, the evidence doesn't matter. Leaders often install new methods on top of old mindsets, then wonder why the change collapses. Methods manage behavior. Mindsets determine it.

If you want different results, you must start upstream — with how people think about their work, their role, and their responsibility.

Mindset as the Bridge Between Human and System

Reliable organizations understand that mindset is the bridge between human leadership and system discipline. Systems give structure; mindsets give meaning. One without the other drifts.

Checks, audits, and communication loops only work when people believe the discipline itself matters. When people see safety or reliability as compliance, they work to avoid blame. When they see it as stewardship, they work to protect value. The process may look identical — but the mindset behind it changes everything.

Belief Before Behavior

Human performance research shows that people act their way into consistency, but believe their way into commitment. Beliefs shape what we notice, how we interpret risk, and what we feel responsible to do.

Change efforts built only on process often trigger resistance. When they begin with mindset, they invite reflection instead of defensiveness. Mindset work slows us down long enough to see our thinking — and once we can see it, we can choose it.

The Role of Reflection

Each day in this series uses reflection because reflection turns belief into evidence. It's easy to agree with a principle; it's harder to see where our own behavior quietly violates it.

The daily structure — The Moment, The Mindset, The Discipline, Reflection, Commitment — surfaces that gap. The goal is not guilt; it's growth. Real change comes from small, repeated recalibrations — a rhythm of awareness.

Evidence-Based Thinking

Mindset work is also evidence work. It replaces assumption with observation and story with pattern. When you treat your own reactions as data, you become both scientist and subject.

Evidence-based leaders look for behavioral patterns and adjust beliefs to match reality. These pages don't give rules; they offer mirrors — invitations to see clarity, consistency, or drift in your own environment.

The Outcome

When mindsets change, everything aligns faster. Communication sharpens. Systems gain purpose. Results finally match intent.

Mindset isn't the warm-up to the work — it *is* the work. It's how you close the gap between what you say and what you show. When leaders change how they think, they don't just create new systems — they create new possibilities.

The Abstract Thinking Framework

The Abstract Thinking Framework is built on the idea that clarity is not a personality trait — it is an engineered system. It consists of **twelve interacting capabilities** that work together to help you absorb, organize, understand, and translate complex ideas.

Each capability strengthens the others.
Together, they form a complete architecture for thinking.

I. FOUNDATION CAPABILITIES

1. Buckets (Categorization)

Purpose: Reduce mental overload by sorting ideas into meaningful categories.

Core Questions:
- What type of idea is this?
- What bucket does it belong to (Principle, Mechanism, Pattern, Behavior, Context)?

Outcome: Thinking begins structured, not chaotic.

2. Scaffolding (Mental Structure-Building)

Purpose: Create a stable frame for a developing idea.

Core Questions:
- What's the backbone of this concept?
- What supports what?

Outcome: Ideas stop collapsing; meaning has a place to grow.

3. Compression (Essence Extraction)

Purpose: Distill a complex idea into its core meaning without losing accuracy.

Core Questions:

- What is essential?
- What would break if removed?

Outcome: The idea becomes portable, memorable, and workable.

II. CLARITY CAPABILITIES

4. Mechanisms (Cause-Based Thinking)

Purpose: Explain how something actually works, not just describe what it does.

Core Questions:
- What makes this happen?
- What's the underlying engine?

Outcome: Deep understanding replaces guesswork.

5. Patterns (Recognition & Predictability)

Purpose: Identify recurring structures across different situations.

Core Questions:
- Where have I seen this before?
- What repeats?

Outcome: Complexity becomes predictable.

6. Layers (Meaning Through Depth)

Purpose: Move from surface information to structural truth.

Core Layers:
- Surface
- Mechanism
- Pattern
- Principle

Outcome: Insight becomes three-dimensional instead of flat.

7. Invisible Forces (Systems Pressure Awareness)

Purpose: Identify incentives, constraints, and pressures shaping behavior or events.

Core Questions:
- What's pushing this to happen?
- What constraints or incentives drive it?

Outcome: You stop misinterpreting symptoms as causes.

III. ACCURACY CAPABILITIES

8. Interrogation (Bias Prevention & Assumption Testing)

Purpose: Protect thinking from mental shortcuts and untested beliefs.

Core Questions:
- What assumption is this resting on?
- What evidence contradicts this?

Outcome: Accuracy improves; bias weakens.

9. Reconstruction (Rebuilding the Idea in Your Own Structure)

Purpose: Convert passive understanding into active mastery.

Core Questions:
- Can I rebuild this idea from scratch?
- Can I explain it without referencing the source?

Outcome: Understanding becomes internal, not borrowed.

10. Systems Thinking (Context and Interaction)

Purpose: Understand how parts interact to create outcomes.

Core Questions:
- What are the inputs, flows, constraints, loops?
- What system produces this result?

Outcome: You stop blaming individuals for system behavior.

IV. INTEGRATION CAPABILITIES

11. Cognitive Models (Blueprints for Reuse)

Purpose: Build reusable mental frameworks that make future learning easier.

Core Questions:
- What structure defines this domain?
- How can this model carry future ideas?

Outcome: The unfamiliar becomes learnable; complexity becomes compact.

12. Translation (Carrying Understanding Across Minds)

Purpose: Turn internal clarity into shared clarity — the ultimate test of understanding.

Core Questions:
- How do I express the mechanism, pattern, and principle cleanly?
- What level of abstraction does the listener need?

Outcome: Understanding becomes influence, leadership, and teaching.

The Meta-Capability: Thinking As A System

When you use these capabilities together:

- Buckets reduce overload
- Scaffolding provides structure
- Compression shapes essence
- Mechanisms reveal truth
- Patterns reveal repetition
- Layers reveal depth
- Invisible forces reveal context
- Interrogation ensures accuracy
- Reconstruction ensures ownership
- Systems thinking reveals why outcomes repeat
- Models create reusability
- Translation creates shared understanding

This is abstract thinking:
a unified system that turns information into comprehension, comprehension into clarity, and clarity into action.

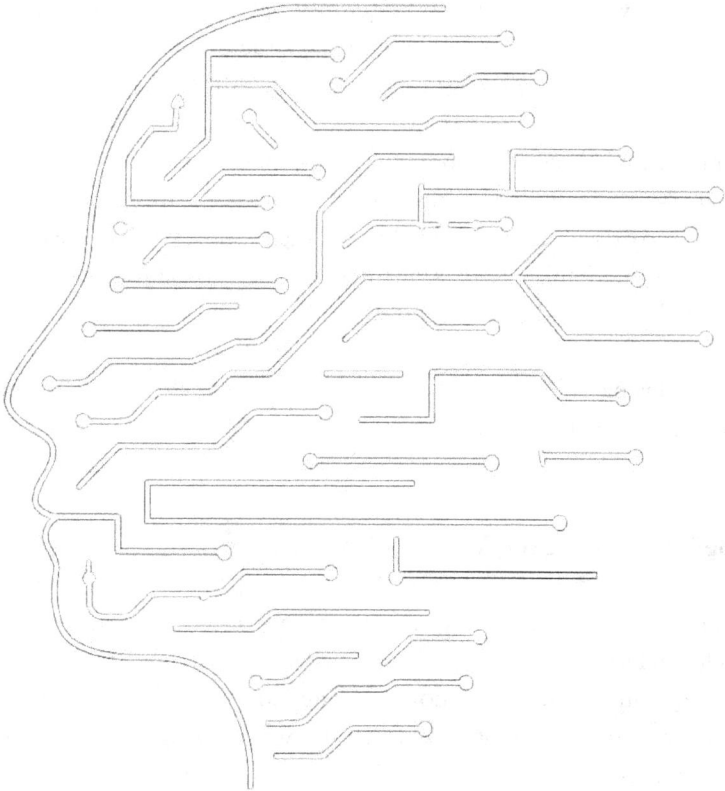

Opening Narrative — Before & After

Why This Opening Narrative Exists

This book is built around thirty days of disciplined practice, but before entering the daily structure it is useful to see what abstract thinking looks like in real conditions. The following short narrative illustrates the difference between operating without a framework and operating with one. It shows the contrast between unstructured interpretation and structured understanding, using a familiar setting most leaders experience regularly.

This example is not the model for your own experience. It is simply a starting point — a reference that helps you recognize the shift you will develop over the next thirty days. As you move through the lessons, you will see the same patterns, mechanisms, and structures revealed in your own work, decisions, conversations, and environments.

Treat this narrative as a baseline: a picture of how clarity changes when thinking is organized with intention.

Before: Operating Without Structure

The leadership meeting began the way it usually did: too much information, delivered too quickly, with meanings embedded in tone, timing, and assumption rather than in structure. A dozen updates competed for attention. Production had a constraint on Line 4. Maintenance was tracking two emerging defects. Planning needed a decision on a late shipment. Everyone spoke as if the connections were obvious, but no one agreed on what the problem actually was.

As the discussion accelerated, interpretations multiplied. Some focused on the behavior of a single department. Others focused on a symptom seen earlier in the week. Decisions formed quickly, but none of them were anchored in a shared understanding. By the end of the meeting, there were three competing explanations for the same event, four unrelated action items, and no clear picture of the mechanism driving the issue. The team left with the feeling of progress, but no confidence in the path forward.

The confusion did not come from lack of intelligence or effort. It came from the absence of a method for slowing information, sorting it, structuring it, and revealing meaning. Without architecture, the mind fills gaps with assumption, habit, and urgency. Complexity becomes noise, and decisions become reactions.

After: Operating With Structure

Weeks later, the same meeting took place — same room, same roles, same operational pressures — but the conversation unfolded differently. The updates were slowed enough to separate signal from noise. Information was sorted into clear buckets: constraint, condition, requirement, risk. Once the updates had a structure, the mechanism behind the issue surfaced almost immediately.

Patterns from previous weeks connected cleanly. A single leverage point became visible. Instead of defending positions, the team examined the system. Instead of reacting to symptoms, they understood the cause-and-effect pathway.

The decision that had once taken an hour of debate was made in minutes, supported by clarity rather than confidence alone.

The meeting felt lighter, calmer, and more disciplined, not because the work had become easier, but because the thinking had become organized. Structure transformed complexity into something navigable. What once felt like noise now felt like a system revealing itself.

This book is designed to create that shift — the movement from unstructured thought to structured clarity, from reacting to understanding, from information to meaning.

The 30-Day Architecture of Structured Thought

The thirty days in this book are not independent lessons. They form a deliberate progression, moving from basic stability to deeper layers of understanding and, finally, to strategic clarity. Each week strengthens a different dimension of thought, building an integrated system you can apply in real time.

Week 1: Stability and Structure

Days 1–7 establish the foundation. You learn to slow information, sort it into buckets, scaffold ideas, compress complexity, and tolerate ambiguity. This creates the internal stability needed for deeper cognitive work.

Week 2: Ordering and Mechanism

Days 8–14 sharpen your ability to see the structure beneath information. You identify mechanisms, recognize patterns, separate metaphor from cause, and work through conflicting interpretations. This week strengthens clarity and precision.

Week 3: Deep Processing and Acceleration

Days 15–21 develop the internal architecture that allows clarity to accelerate. You learn to interrogate ideas, connect new concepts to what you know, hold unfinished meaning, extend your capacity into unfamiliar domains, and work across layers of insight.

Week 4: Strategic Understanding and Application

Days 22–30 move from insight to application. You learn to see invisible forces, navigate meaning across layers, turn understanding into action, recognize principles in motion, simplify without distortion, and operate as someone who stabilizes meaning for others.

The System as a Whole

Across the thirty days, you build a method for transforming complexity into clarity. The skills progress from foundational (sorting, slowing, scaffolding) to structural (mechanism, pattern, layering) to advanced (translation, simplification, strategic insight). The model is cumulative: each layer strengthens the next, and the system becomes more natural with repetition.

This meta-model serves as a map for the month and a reference you can return to whenever you need to stabilize your thinking or re-enter the system.

Day 1 — Thinking Is a Skill, Not a Trait

The Lesson

Most people grow up believing that thinking — real thinking — is something you either "have" or "don't." We talk about people as if they are naturally sharp or naturally slow, as if clarity were a personality trait instead of a trained ability. That quiet assumption does real damage. If you believe your thinking is fixed, you never challenge it. You accept confusion as permanent. You work around problems instead of working through them. You downgrade what you are capable of long before reality ever gets a vote.

Thinking is not a gift. Thinking is a skill. Your brain rewires itself across a lifetime in response to what you regularly ask it to do. If you feed it fragments, it becomes good at jumping to conclusions. If you feed it noise, it becomes restless and scattered. But if you consistently ask it to slow down, to organize, to search for mechanism and principle, it becomes structurally better at that work. Over time, your mind learns to hold more complexity, to separate signal from decoration, and to see the pattern running underneath the details.

This book is about that upgrade. You are not here to collect clever ideas or inspirational phrases. You are here to rebuild the way you think — the habits, the structures, and the disciplines that sit underneath every decision you make. Across the next thirty days, you will practice consuming ideas more deliberately, codifying what you see, and translating abstraction into clear, usable meaning. Thinking is not an accident. It is an operating system. Today you stop treating it as something you were given and start treating it as something you are responsible for building. As you move through these pages, the goal is not perfection. The goal is to become a person who takes ownership of their own thinking, who understands that every day is another repetition in the craft of understanding.

The Reflection

Where in your life have you assumed your thinking was fixed? Perhaps in subjects you avoid, conversations you dread, or decisions that feel heavy and mentally expensive. How has that belief shaped your confidence, your curiosity, or the kinds of challenges you are even willing to attempt?

Now think of a time when you did improve at something complex — a new role, a technical concept, a difficult conversation, a sport or craft. At the beginning it felt awkward, effortful, maybe even intimidating. Over time, with repetition and structure, it became easier and more natural. What changed was not the task; what changed was your brain's ability to handle it.

Those experiences are proof that your thinking is already more flexible than you give it credit for. Reflect on what might shift in the next thirty days if you treated thinking not as a fixed trait, but as a discipline you are consciously training, one deliberate repetition at a time.

The Commitment

- I will treat thinking as a skill I can build.
- I will slow down enough to understand.
- I will approach complex ideas with curiosity instead of avoidance.
- I will give myself permission to grow.

EBR Principle

Clarity isn't inherited — it's built. When you train your thinking, you expand your capacity.

Day 2 — Slowing Input to Increase Understanding

The Lesson

Most people take in information faster than their mind can organize it. We skim emails, half-listen to conversations, scroll through ideas, and then wonder why nothing stays long enough to form real understanding. The issue isn't intelligence — it's pace. Your mind cannot build structure around information that passes through too quickly. When input outruns processing, all you're left with is fragments, impressions, and a vague sense of mental clutter that feels busy but empty.

Slowing input is not about moving through life at a crawl. It's about giving your brain enough time to do the work that actually leads to comprehension: sorting, grouping, connecting, and codifying what it encounters. When you pause after a sentence or reread a paragraph, you're not stalling — you're building understanding. You're allowing your mind to notice the mechanism beneath the surface, to pick up the pattern underneath the details, and to position the idea inside your existing conceptual structure instead of letting it drift past.

This practice becomes even more important as ideas grow more abstract. Complex concepts can't be absorbed at the speed they are delivered. They have to be digested at the speed your mind can meaningfully process them. Leaders often feel pressure to keep pace with information rather than master it, especially in fast-moving meetings, inboxes, and dashboards. But abstraction doesn't reward speed — it rewards precision. Slowing down the input is what ultimately accelerates comprehension. Once your mind has built the right internal scaffolding, ideas begin to click faster, connect faster, and make sense faster. Depth first, speed second. That is the real path to cognitive clarity and confident judgment. Over time, this way of consuming information becomes its own habit. You stop chasing every phrase and start listening for structure. You notice repeats, contradictions, and missing pieces. You realize that most confusion was never about your ability; it was about the pace you were forcing your mind to endure.

The Reflection

Where do you feel the strongest pull to consume information too quickly? Maybe in meetings where you're trying to keep up, in conversations where ideas come faster than you can process, or when reading material that feels dense or unfamiliar. How does that pressure shape your actual understanding, not just your sense of staying caught up?

Now recall a moment when you deliberately slowed the input — rereading something, asking a clarifying question, replaying a conversation in your mind, or breaking an idea into smaller parts. What did you notice only after you gave the idea room to breathe? What clicked that hadn't clicked before? Consider how often insight has been lost in your world not because the idea was too complex, but because the pace was too fast for your mind to capture, organize, and keep it. Imagine what might change in your work, your learning, and your leadership if you treated pacing as a lever for clarity instead of a race to keep up.

The Commitment

- I will reduce speed to increase understanding.
- I will choose clarity over pace.
- I will pause long enough for ideas to form structure.
- I will give my mind time to do its best work.

EBR Principle

Slow the input. Grow the understanding.

Day 3 — Conceptual Buckets

The Lesson

One of the quiet challenges of abstract thinking is that the mind doesn't know where to put new ideas. When concepts arrive without a place to land, they drift. They feel overwhelming, slippery, or disconnected from anything familiar. This isn't a sign of low intelligence — it's a sign of missing structure. The mind needs buckets, categories, and containers to hold meaning. Without them, everything feels equally important and equally confusing. With them, complexity begins to sort itself out.

Conceptual buckets are not about reducing ideas to something shallow. They are about giving the mind somewhere to begin. When you encounter a new idea, the first question isn't "Do I understand this?" but rather "What kind of thing is this?" Is it a principle? A mechanism? A pattern? A behavior? A system? A decision input? A constraint? Once you sort the idea into its bucket, the mind snaps into alignment. You immediately gain a sense of what matters, what to compare it to, and how it should connect to the rest of your thinking.

As you move through this book, you will build your own set of buckets — the categories that make sense for how you lead, learn, and solve problems. These buckets will become the scaffolding that holds your understanding together. Every abstract thinker relies on them. They allow you to compress complexity, spot inconsistencies, and translate ideas into language others can grasp. You aren't trying to force ideas into rigid boxes; you're giving them a home so your mind can work on them with precision instead of chaos. Once you have reliable buckets, new concepts stop feeling like puzzles scattered across a table and start feeling like pieces that actually belong somewhere. That shift is where clarity begins.

The Reflection

What ideas in your world feel hardest to hold onto? Are they strategic concepts, people issues, system interactions, cultural patterns, or technical mechanisms? Notice whether the difficulty comes from the idea itself or from the absence of a clear category to place it in. The mind struggles most when it has nowhere to set something down. Confusion is often not a failure of comprehension but a failure of placement.

Think back to times when a confusing idea suddenly clicked simply because you recognized what "kind" of idea it was. Maybe a behavior made sense once you saw it as a pattern rather than an isolated event. Maybe a decision became clearer when you realized it was governed by a principle, not a preference. These moments reveal how much clarity depends on classification — on giving ideas a place to live.

Now consider which conceptual buckets already exist in your thinking, even if you've never formally named them. You may already sort things into systems, incentives, behaviors, or root causes without realizing it.

This practice builds the foundation you will refine throughout the book as you begin using categories to stabilize meaning.

The Commitment

- I will sort ideas before trying to understand them.
- I will build categories that help my mind stay organized.
- I will resist the urge to treat every detail as equal.
- I will give new concepts a place to belong.

EBR Principle

Understanding begins with sorting. Once an idea has a home, clarity can follow.

Day 4 — Mental Scaffolding

The Lesson

Every complex structure requires support, and your thinking is no different. Mental scaffolding is the internal framework that holds ideas in place long enough for you to examine them, compare them, and understand how they fit together. Without scaffolding, new concepts feel slippery or chaotic. Even when the idea itself is not difficult, your mind has no stable platform from which to work on it. With scaffolding, the same idea becomes manageable. You can anchor it, rotate it, and connect it to what you already know.

Scaffolding doesn't appear all at once. It develops through repetition — through the consistent act of encountering ideas, grouping them, codifying them, and revisiting them until the underlying structure begins to reveal itself. As you build scaffolding, your mind becomes better at organizing complexity. You stop trying to hold every detail at once and start relying on the framework you've built. Over time, this framework becomes your intellectual home — the place where meaning is constructed, where confusion is resolved, and where abstract ideas become usable.

This book will help you strengthen that scaffolding day by day. Each lesson introduces a new beam, a new cross-brace, a new support that allows your mind to hold more weight than it could before. You are not trying to remember every concept; you are trying to build the structure that makes remembering unnecessary. Strong scaffolding is what allows experienced thinkers to engage with complexity calmly. They are not less intimidated by big ideas; they are simply better supported by the frameworks they have built over time. That same support system is available to you. The more scaffolding you create, the more your mind becomes a place where ideas can take shape instead of slipping away.

The Reflection

What subjects or conversations tend to collapse on you when you try to think through them? Notice whether the problem is actually the idea itself, or the absence of a stable internal framework to hold it. Consider how often you've abandoned a complex idea not because it was beyond your ability, but because you lacked the scaffolding to support it.

Now reflect on a time when a topic *did* become easier for you — perhaps a technical concept, a leadership skill, or a pattern in people's behavior. What changed? It wasn't the topic. It was the structure you gradually built through exposure, repetition, and reflection. That structure allowed you to carry more cognitive weight with less effort.

As you move through this book, pay attention to the pieces of scaffolding you already possess and the pieces you still need to build. Understanding improves dramatically when your mind has a place to set things down. What new supports would make the ideas in your world easier to hold, easier to work with, and easier to understand?

The Commitment

- I will build internal structures that support complex ideas.
- I will revisit concepts until the scaffolding becomes strong.
- I will not confuse lack of structure with lack of ability.
- I will give my mind the supports it needs to think clearly.

EBR Principle

Strong thinking requires strong scaffolding. Build the structure, and clarity will follow.

Day 5 — Cognitive Compression

The Lesson

As ideas grow more complex, the mind needs a way to reduce them without distorting them. This is the function of cognitive compression — the ability to shrink a large concept into a smaller, clearer form while preserving its essence. People who struggle with abstract thinking often feel overwhelmed because they try to hold every detail at once. But experienced thinkers don't handle more information; they handle information differently. They compress it. They extract the principle, the mechanism, or the pattern that makes the details meaningful. Once the core is clear, the details fall into place.

Compression is not simplification for convenience. It is simplification for understanding. When you compress an idea, you are not weakening it; you are strengthening your ability to work with it. A compressed idea is easier to recall, easier to compare, and far easier to translate to others. Leaders who cannot compress their thinking often drown their teams in unnecessary detail. Leaders who *can* compress their thinking create clarity, direction, and alignment without sacrificing accuracy. Compression is one of the most powerful intellectual tools you can develop.

This book will repeatedly train you to find the core of an idea and articulate it cleanly. You will practice distilling paragraphs into sentences, sentences into principles, and principles into usable meaning. Over time, this skill becomes automatic. You automatically look for the mechanism instead of the noise. You automatically search for the governing rule instead of the distracting exception. And you automatically build your understanding from the inside out, starting with the principle rather than the detail. Cognitive compression is what makes abstraction workable. It allows you to carry more insight with less effort — the mental equivalent of packing a complex machine into a compact, well-engineered design that still performs flawlessly.

The Reflection

What ideas in your world feel too "big" to hold all at once? Notice whether the difficulty comes from the idea itself or from attempting to manage too many details without identifying the principle that unites them. Think back to a time when a complex situation finally clicked because you realized the underlying rule or pattern. Once that core was clear, everything else fell into place.

Now consider how often misunderstanding arises in your work because people focus on the details rather than the structure. How much conflict, confusion, or wasted motion comes from talking about symptoms instead of principles? As you move forward, pay attention to the moments when compression brings relief — when naming the central concept suddenly makes the entire situation easier to understand. Compression is not just a cognitive tool; it is a leadership skill. It determines how clearly you think, how clearly you communicate, and how clearly others can follow.

Compression is a core element of the framework; today's work brings it into the level of daily thinking and decision-making.

The Commitment

- I will look for the principle before the detail.
- I will practice shrinking ideas without losing their meaning.
- I will use compression to create clarity for myself and others.
- I will treat complexity as something to organize, not fear.

EBR Principle

Find the core. Name it clearly. Let everything else take its place.

Day 6 — Tolerating Ambiguity

The Lesson

One of the most important skills in abstract thinking is the ability to tolerate ambiguity — to hold an idea that is not yet finished without rushing to force it into clarity. Most people experience unfinished understanding as discomfort. They want answers now, certainty now, structure now. The mind craves closure, even if the closure is inaccurate or shallow. But abstraction rarely reveals itself all at once. It emerges in layers, patterns, contradictions, and slow-forming connections. If you cannot tolerate ambiguity, you cannot understand complexity.

Ambiguity tolerance is not passive. It is an active discipline. It means allowing your mind to sit inside the question instead of sprinting toward an outcome. It means resisting the urge to simplify too soon, to decide too soon, or to declare something "understood" before the understanding is real. Leaders who lack this discipline often force decisions prematurely. They cling to the first explanation they can articulate instead of holding the space needed for deeper clarity. Their thinking feels fast, but it is actually shallow.

When you learn to tolerate ambiguity, something powerful happens: your brain stops panicking in the presence of the unknown. You stop confusing uncertainty with incompetence. You stop mistaking discomfort for danger. And you give your mind the necessary room to discover patterns, principles, and mechanisms that cannot be seen in the first few seconds of looking. Ambiguity tolerance is not about enjoying confusion — it is about recognizing that confusion is often the doorway to understanding. The thinkers who see the deepest are the ones willing to stand inside the fog just a little longer, trusting that clarity will form if they do not rush the process. This skill is not emotional; it is structural. It teaches your mind to work at the depth that complexity requires.

The Reflection

Where in your life do you feel the strongest urge to resolve uncertainty immediately? Notice whether that impulse comes from the situation itself or from the internal discomfort of "not knowing." Think about the last time you rushed into an explanation simply because the silence or ambiguity felt too uncomfortable to hold. What insights emerged later — insights you could have reached earlier if you had waited just a little longer?

Now remember a moment when you stayed with ambiguity rather than forcing a quick answer. Perhaps you were evaluating a decision, coaching someone, diagnosing a problem, or trying to understand a complex topic. What did patience allow you to see? What patterns or principles emerged only after the initial fog began to clear? Consider how different your work and leadership might feel if you treated ambiguity not as a threat, but as the raw material from which clarity is built.

The Commitment

- I will resist the urge to rush clarity.
- I will give my mind time to work beneath the surface.
- I will treat ambiguity as a stage of understanding, not a failure.
- I will practice standing inside the unknown without panic.

EBR Principle

Clarity grows in the space you refuse to rush.

Day 7 — Week 1 Practice Lab (Practice Day #1)

The Lesson

You have spent six days building the foundations of abstract thinking: slowing input, creating conceptual buckets, building scaffolding, compressing ideas, and tolerating ambiguity. Today is about turning those concepts into practice. Abstract thinking is not learned by reading alone — it is learned by doing. These exercises train your mind to hold, organize, compress, and reinterpret ideas with greater clarity and less effort. Treat today as a workout for your thinking architecture. Move slowly, stay curious, and let the structure do the work.

Exercise 1 — Conceptual Bucket Sort

Choose **one paragraph** from anything you are currently reading — a memo, an article, a book.

1. Read it slowly.
2. Sort the major ideas into buckets: *principle, mechanism, detail, pattern, behavior, or context.*
3. Notice which ideas suddenly become clearer simply because they have a place to belong.

Exercise 2 — 2-Sentence Compression Drill

- Take a complex idea you heard or read this week.
- Compress it into **two sentences** without losing meaning.
- Ask yourself: *What is the essence? What is noise?*

Exercise 3 — Scaffolding Builder

Take a topic you find confusing. Sketch a simple scaffold for it:
- What are the pillars?
- What holds it together?
- What sits on top of what?
  If you can draw its structure, you can understand it.

Exercise 4 — Ambiguity Hold
1. Set a timer for **60 seconds**.
2. Choose a question you don't yet know the answer to.
3. Sit with it — no rushing, no conclusions.
4. Notice how your mind reacts.
5. Your only job is to tolerate the unfinished shape of the idea.

The Reflection

Which exercise felt easiest for you, and which felt the hardest? What does that reveal about the way your mind naturally organizes (or resists) structure? Did slowing down a paragraph reveal anything you missed the first time? Did compressing an idea bring unexpected clarity? Did ambiguity feel uncomfortable, or did it feel like an invitation to deeper thinking? Consider which of today's exercises you want to revisit regularly — not as tasks, but as training for a mind that is becoming more capable, more organized, and more precise.

The Commitment

- I will practice the disciplines that strengthen my thinking.
- I will value structure as much as insight.
- I will revisit these exercises until they feel natural.
- I will treat today's work as the beginning of deeper clarity.

EBR Principle

Thinking sharpens through repetition — one disciplined rep at a time.

Day 8 — How the Mind Sorts Information

The Lesson

Every moment of your day, your mind is flooded with information — conversations, signals, impressions, data, expectations, contradictions, and patterns. If your brain tried to process all of this equally, you would collapse under the weight of it. The reason you don't is because your mind is constantly sorting, categorizing, filtering, and prioritizing what it encounters. This sorting process is not random, and it is not automatic in the way most people assume. It is a learned system. And the more intentionally you shape it, the more powerful your thinking becomes.

At the core of this sorting mechanism are three disciplines: **categorization, codification, and sequencing**. Categorization determines the broad nature of an idea — what type of thing it is. Codification assigns the idea to a meaningful group, clarifying its purpose, its role, and its relationship to the whole. Sequencing reveals order: what drives what, what depends on what, what comes first, and what only appears important until you understand the deeper structure beneath it. Together, these disciplines shape how quickly and accurately you can understand complex situations.

Most people struggle not because they lack intelligence, but because they lack a reliable sorting system. They treat every signal as equally important. They react to noise as if it were structure. They drown in details because nothing has been assigned a proper category. But once your mind begins sorting information deliberately, complexity stops feeling chaotic and starts feeling navigable. You begin seeing the "shape" of situations more quickly — the way ideas relate, the way causes stack beneath effects, the way behaviors reveal incentives, the way decisions depend on hidden patterns. Sorting is not a luxury of advanced thinkers; it is the *source* of their clarity. When your mind knows how to organize what it encounters, understanding accelerates.

The Reflection

Think back to the last time you felt overwhelmed by information — maybe in a meeting, a project discussion, or a decision with too many moving parts. What made it overwhelming? Was it truly the complexity of the issue, or was it the lack of categories to sort the incoming signals? Now consider a time when clarity emerged suddenly, not because the information changed, but because *you* changed the way you organized it. Perhaps you realized what the real driver was, or you saw a pattern in what had looked like unrelated details.

What does this tell you about the power of sorting? Notice whether your mind tends to jump to detail or to structure, to reaction or to categories. Over the next few days, pay attention to your internal sorting process. Where does information go when it enters your mind? Does it fall into place, or does it scatter? The more conscious you become of your sorting habits, the more control you gain over how you understand the world around you.

This expands the work from Day 3 by shifting from identifying categories to using them in real time to control complexity.

The Commitment

- I will sort information before reacting to it.
- I will identify the type, purpose, and order of what I encounter.
- I will treat complexity as something that can be organized.
- I will strengthen the structures that support clear thinking.

EBR Principle

When your mind sorts well, you see well. Clarity begins with order.

Day 9 — Mechanism Over Metaphor

The Lesson

Most people understand the world through stories, metaphors, and surface impressions. These aren't wrong — metaphors can help simplify something unfamiliar — but they can also obscure what actually matters. Abstract thinkers operate differently. They look past the metaphor to find the mechanism: the underlying structure that makes something work, fail, behave, or repeat. When you understand the mechanism, you understand the idea. When you rely only on the metaphor, your understanding is fragile and collapses the moment the analogy no longer fits.

Mechanisms are the engines beneath the surface. They reveal cause-and-effect relationships, dependencies, drivers, constraints, and predictable outcomes. If you understand the mechanism behind a behavior, you can anticipate it. If you understand the mechanism behind a system, you can improve it. If you understand the mechanism behind a failure, you can prevent it. Mechanisms give you leverage — the ability to think accurately and act decisively without guessing. They offer clarity where metaphors offer comfort.

In your daily work, you will encounter countless moments when the explanation that sounds satisfying is not the explanation that is true. People will offer stories about why something happened, but stories are not mechanisms. Explanations built on metaphor may feel intuitive, but intuition without structure leads to misalignment, poor decisions, and repeated mistakes. Looking for the mechanism forces you to move past assumption and into accuracy. It disciplines your thinking to ask: *What is actually happening underneath this? What drives it? What governs it? What repeats?* When you train your mind to search for the mechanism first, everything else lines up more cleanly — the categories, the patterns, the principles, the predictions, and the actions. Metaphors help you explain things. Mechanisms help you understand them. And understanding is always the stronger foundation.

The Reflection

Think of a recent situation that frustrated you — a conversation, a decision, a conflict, or a repeating issue in your work or personal life. How did you interpret it at the time? Were you relying on a metaphor or story about what must be happening, or did you examine the underlying mechanism? Now imagine looking at that situation again with new questions: *What incentive drove this? What constraint shaped it? What system produced it? What sequence led to it?* Notice how different the situation feels when you search for what actually governs it rather than what merely explains it.

Reflect on how often misunderstandings in your world come from confusing metaphor with mechanism — from accepting the comfortable story instead of uncovering the machinery beneath it. Over the next few days, challenge yourself to pause whenever you feel certain you "already understand." Certainty is often the first sign that you are leaning on a metaphor instead of a mechanism. True understanding requires deeper work.

The Commitment

- I will look beneath the story for the structure.
- I will ask what drives something before I ask how it feels.
- I will explain things only after I understand their mechanism.
- I will treat metaphor as a tool, not a substitute for thinking.

EBR Principle

Metaphors explain. Mechanisms reveal. Choose the layer that leads to truth.

Day 10 — Cause → Pattern → Principle

The Lesson

Every abstract thinker learns to see the world through three layers: causes, patterns, and principles. These layers form a ladder of understanding — each rung giving you a clearer and more stable view of whatever you are trying to make sense of. At the lowest layer is **cause**, the concrete event or driver that produces an outcome. Above that is **pattern**, the repetition or regularity that emerges when individual causes stack in similar ways. At the highest layer is **principle**, the rule or truth that governs why the pattern exists at all. Most people live at the cause level, reacting to events as if each one is new. But abstraction begins when you climb higher.

When you learn to recognize patterns, you stop treating every moment as unique. You begin to see the familiar echoes in different situations — the way certain behaviors predict certain outcomes, the way incentives shape choices, the way systems repeat themselves even when the people inside them change. Patterns give you foresight. They allow you to anticipate what will happen next without waiting for it to confirm itself. But patterns are not the final destination of thinking; they are the bridge to something deeper.

The real power comes from understanding **principle**: the governing rule that makes the pattern predictable. When you understand the principle, you can diagnose problems faster, make decisions with more confidence, and teach others with more clarity. Principles allow you to compress complexity into a clean, stable framework that travels across situations and contexts. As you move through this book, your goal is not simply to see causes or even patterns — it is to extract the principle that sits above them. Causes reveal what happened. Patterns reveal what often happens. Principles reveal what must happen unless something changes. The higher you climb, the clearer everything becomes.

The Reflection

Think of a challenge you've faced recently — perhaps a recurring issue with a colleague, a recurring failure in a system, or a personal habit you want to change. Did you focus on the immediate cause, or did you look for the pattern beneath it? And if a pattern existed, did you take the final step of identifying the principle that governed it? Now explore what would shift if you framed that situation through this three-tiered lens.

Consider how often you have solved the cause but left the pattern intact because the principle driving it remained hidden. Reflect on the problems in your world that no longer surprise you — the ones you can predict with uncanny accuracy. What principle explains their consistency? As you think through this, pay attention to how your mind climbs the ladder: from event to repetition to rule. This movement is the essence of abstraction, and the more consciously you practice it, the more natural it becomes.

The Commitment

- I will search for patterns instead of reacting to isolated events.
- I will identify the principle behind the pattern.
- I will use principles to navigate complexity with clarity.
- I will climb the ladder of understanding, not stay at the surface.

EBR Principle

Causes explain the moment. Principles explain the truth.

Day 11 — Thinking in Systems

<u>The Lesson</u>

Most people think in straight lines: A causes B, B causes C, and so on. But the world rarely behaves in straight lines. It behaves in systems — interconnected structures where causes loop back on themselves, where actions create unintended consequences, and where problems rarely stay contained in the place they began. When you learn to think in systems, you stop treating every issue as isolated. You begin to see how events, incentives, constraints, behaviors, and environments form a web of relationships that produce the outcomes you observe. Systems thinking doesn't just explain what is happening; it explains why it keeps happening.

Systems reveal themselves when you look beyond the obvious signal to the structure beneath it. Every persistent problem is supported by a system. Every repeating success is supported by a system. Every cultural trait — good or bad — is supported by a system. When you treat events as independent, you miss the reinforcing loops, the delays, the hidden feedback, and the downstream effects that shape the system's behavior. But when you begin to map relationships instead of reactions, clarity emerges. You see which components matter most, which forces amplify each other, and where the leverage points actually are.

System thinkers are not smarter; they are simply looking at more of the picture. They know that changing one part of a system often changes the whole system, and not always in predictable ways. They pay attention to how information moves, how decisions cascade, how incentives distort behavior, and how bottlenecks form. They treat symptoms as signals, not answers. The more you practice thinking in systems, the more you begin to recognize that complexity is not random — it is structured. And when something is structured, it can be understood, influenced, and improved. Systems thinking is not a different type of intelligence. It is a different type of attention.

The Reflection

Think of a recurring issue in your workplace or personal life — something that shows up again and again despite attempts to address it. How have you been interpreting it? As an isolated problem, or as a pattern produced by a system? What relationships, incentives, or constraints might be shaping it beneath the surface? Now consider what would change if you stopped trying to "fix the event" and instead examined the structure producing the event.

Reflect on a time when solving one problem accidentally created another. What system connections were you unaware of at the time? How might your decision have been different if you had mapped the relationships between the factors involved? Systems thinking isn't about building complicated diagrams; it's about training your attention to look for interdependence rather than isolation. As you move forward, pay attention to what changes when you start asking not just "What happened?" but "What system made this possible?"

The Commitment

- I will look for structure beneath every repeating event.
- I will treat problems as system outputs, not isolated moments.
- I will identify the relationships that shape behavior and outcomes.
- I will use systems thinking to find leverage, not blame.

EBR Principle

Nothing stands alone. Systems create the outcomes you see.

Day 12 — Working Memory Strength

The Lesson

Working memory is the mental workspace where you hold, compare, and manipulate ideas before they are stored, understood, or acted on. It is not the same as intelligence. It is not the same as memory. It is the "clearing on the table" where complex thinking happens. When working memory is overloaded, ideas blur together, details slip, and confusion rises. When working memory is strong, you can hold multiple concepts at once, see their relationships, test interpretations, and build structure without losing your place. Most people underestimate how central this skill is to abstract thinking — and how trainable it actually is.

Working memory becomes strained not because a person is incapable, but because too many ideas are entering the mind without organization. When concepts are unsorted, uncategorized, or uncompressed, they take up far more space than necessary. But when ideas have buckets, scaffolding, and principles attached to them, they shrink down to manageable units. A person with strong working memory isn't storing more information; they're storing well-organized information. The mind can juggle far more when each idea has been prepared properly.

Strengthening working memory does not happen through willpower alone. It happens through repetition — through the daily practice of slowing input, sorting ideas, compressing principles, and tolerating ambiguity long enough for structure to form. Over time, your mental workspace becomes more spacious, more stable, and more efficient. You stop losing your place in complex discussions. You stop feeling overwhelmed when multiple variables shift at once. You stop abandoning abstract ideas simply because they require more temporary cognitive load. Working memory strength is not about becoming superhuman; it is about removing the friction that makes thinking harder than it needs to be. When your internal workspace expands, so does your confidence in navigating complexity.

The Reflection

Think about a moment recently when you felt mentally overloaded — perhaps during a meeting, while learning a new skill, or while trying to hold too many details at once. What actually caused the overwhelm? Was it the amount of information, or the way the information was structured? Now consider a time when you felt mentally steady even in a complex situation. What was different? Did you have clearer categories? A clearer purpose? A clearer sequence? That structure was supporting your working memory.

As you move through this book, pay attention to what makes your mental workspace feel spacious and what makes it feel crowded. Notice whether you treat working memory as something fixed, or as something you can expand through discipline. Reflect on the possibility that many of your limitations in thinking were never about ability — they were about cognitive bandwidth. What becomes possible when that bandwidth grows?

Although this practice involves sorting, its purpose is different: you are strengthening the architecture that supports reasoning under load.

The Commitment

• I will strengthen my mental workspace through daily practice.
• I will organize ideas so they take up less cognitive space.
• I will build habits that reduce overwhelm and increase clarity.
• I will treat working memory as a skill I can expand.

EBR Principle

A larger workspace creates a larger capacity to understand.

Day 13 — Reconstruction Over Recall (Practice Day #2)

The Lesson

Reconstruction is the skill that separates surface-level familiarity from true understanding. Most people rely on recall — repeating information in the same form it was presented. But recall is fragile. It collapses under pressure, fades quickly, and rarely leads to insight. Reconstruction, on the other hand, forces the mind to rebuild the idea from the inside out. It asks you to identify the structure, the mechanism, the principle, and the logic — and then express it in your own language. That process is where comprehension actually occurs.

Reconstruction strengthens the architecture of your thinking. It turns information into knowledge, knowledge into clarity, and clarity into something you can use, explain, or teach. Today's exercises will train your mind to operate at that deeper level — not by memorizing ideas, but by rebuilding them.

Exercise 1 — One-Sentence Compression
- Select a paragraph from anything you read this week.
- Rewrite it as **one sentence** without losing meaning.
- If you can compress it cleanly, you understand it.
- If you can't, reread the paragraph — the structure is still unclear.

Exercise 2 — Three-Layer Meaning Map
Choose a concept you're working on right now.
Map it in three layers:
1. **Surface:** What it appears to be.
2. **Structure:** How it works underneath.
3. **Principle:** Why it behaves this way.
   This reveals the core logic the mind normally misses.

Exercise 3 — The Teaching Test

- Explain a complex idea to an imaginary audience in **three sentences**.
- No metaphors, no jargon — only mechanism.
- If you can teach it cleanly, you understand it.
- If you stumble, rebuild it again.

The Reflection

Which exercise challenged you the most — compression, mapping, or teaching? What does that struggle reveal about how you typically process information? Many people discover that they understand far less than they assumed once they try to compress or teach an idea. That realization is not discouraging; it is clarifying. It shows where your scaffolding is strong and where it needs reinforcement.

Think back on a recent idea, project, or discussion where you felt unsure whether you truly understood what was happening. Would reconstruction have helped? Would forcing yourself to find the principle — or articulate the mechanism — have cut through the fog? As you move through the coming weeks, pay attention to the difference between remembering something and reconstructing it. One is passive. The other is transformative.

The Commitment

- I will rebuild ideas, not simply recall them.
- I will look for the structure beneath the surface.
- I will practice expressing ideas in my own clear language.
- I will use reconstruction to strengthen my thinking every day.

EBR Principle

You don't understand an idea until you can rebuild it.

46

Day 14 — Week 2 Practice Lab (Practice Day #3)

The Lesson

This week introduced some of the deepest structural tools in abstract thinking: seeing mechanisms beneath metaphors, recognizing patterns beneath events, understanding systems beneath problems, and strengthening the working memory that holds it all together. These skills are not theoretical; they reshape the way you interpret everything around you. Today is your chance to practice them deliberately. Each exercise is designed to stretch your mental architecture — to help you see what drives behavior, what repeats, what connects, and what the system behind the moment is trying to reveal.

Thinking at this level requires the mind to stay organized while holding multiple ideas at once. That's why today's work is challenging. You're training yourself to look deeper, connect more precisely, and resist the urge to settle for surface-level explanations. Treat this session as cognitive strength training. The goal is not perfection. The goal is to build the internal machinery that will support every advanced skill you develop in the weeks ahead.

Exercise 1 — Mechanism Identification Drill

Select a recent decision, success, failure, or conflict. Ask:

- *What actually caused this?*
- *What repeated?*
- *What mechanism explains the outcome?*

Write the mechanism in **two clean sentences**.

Exercise 2 — System Sketch

Choose a recurring issue at work or home.

Draw a quick sketch of the system:

- Key forces
- Dependencies
- Feedback loops

- Delays
  You do not need artistic skill — just structure.
  Identify the **one leverage point** that would shift the entire system.

Exercise 3 — Pattern Extraction
- Take five examples of anything that frustrates or puzzles you.
- List them.
- Now circle what is consistent across all five.
- This is the pattern — the truth hiding beneath the noise.

The Reflection

Which exercise stretched your mind the most — identifying mechanisms, sketching systems, or extracting patterns? What does that reveal about the parts of your thinking that are already strong and the parts still developing? When you search for the mechanism or map the system, frustration often dissolves into clarity. Ambiguities become structures. Problems become patterns.

Now reflect on how these tools could reshape the way you approach real situations this week. What would change in a meeting, a conversation, or a decision if you paused long enough to identify the mechanism or map the system? How much mental stress comes from trying to solve problems at the surface instead of the structure beneath them?

The Commitment

- I will search for mechanisms before reacting to moments.
- I will look for system structure beneath recurring problems.
- I will train my mind to extract patterns from noise.
- I will expand my working memory through deliberate practice.

EBR Principle

Look deeper, and thinking gets easier.

Day 15 — The Acceleration Effect

The Lesson

Every discipline eventually reaches a point where practice transforms effort into efficiency. Musicians begin playing passages that once felt impossible. Athletes execute movements that once required conscious focus. Skilled thinkers experience the same shift. What felt slow, heavy, or mentally expensive in the early stages begins to move with surprising speed. This is the acceleration effect — the moment when your repeated exposure to abstraction builds enough structure, familiarity, and cognitive strength that complex ideas no longer feel complex.

Your brain is constantly optimizing itself. Each time you categorize an idea, compress a concept, tolerate ambiguity, or reconstruct meaning, you are strengthening neural pathways that make those processes faster the next time. What originally took minutes begins to take seconds. What once felt overwhelming begins to feel familiar. You're not thinking less — you're thinking more efficiently, because your mind is no longer starting from zero. It now has scaffolding, buckets, patterns, principles, and systems ready to receive new information the moment it arrives.

This acceleration does not come from forcing speed. It comes from repeatedly practicing clarity. As your mental architecture expands, the mind stops getting lost in detail and starts moving directly toward structure. You anticipate patterns earlier. You identify mechanisms more quickly. You sort information more accurately. You recover clarity faster when confusion appears. Over time, you become someone who processes abstraction with a confidence that looks like talent but is, in reality, the product of disciplined practice. The more you work with complex ideas, the faster and easier they become. Cognitive acceleration is not a gift — it is a reward for building a strong foundation and using it consistently.

The Reflection

Think of a skill in your life that once felt difficult but now feels natural —
something you no longer have to consciously "think through" step by step.
How did that shift happen? It wasn't magic. It was repetition, structure, and
increased familiarity. Now apply that same lens to your thinking: what kinds of
ideas already feel easier than they once did? What insights come faster now that
you've built buckets, scaffolding, and the habit of seeking mechanisms and
principles?

Reflect on what this means for the next fifteen days. You are beginning the
second half of the book with more cognitive strength than you had at the start.
What once felt slow will begin to accelerate. The work will change — not
because the ideas become simpler, but because *you* are becoming structurally
stronger. Consider what thinking could feel like for you six months from now if
you continue this discipline.

This is the natural progression of the skills from Days 1–14; structure practiced
consistently becomes speed without loss of clarity. This is the moment when
structure transforms into speed, marking the shift from deliberate practice to
natural clarity.

The Commitment

- I will notice where structure already creates speed in my thinking and
  reinforce it through deliberate practice.
- I will slow down first, then observe where acceleration naturally
  returns.
- I will protect clarity as it emerges, not rush to fill space with
  assumption.

EBR Principle

Practice builds structure. Structure builds speed.

Day 16 — Interrogating Ideas

The Lesson

Clear thinking does not come from consuming ideas; it comes from interrogating them. Most people accept information at face value. They nod along, assume meaning, or rely on intuition to fill the gaps. But abstract thinkers know that understanding is not passive. It is an active process of questioning — of pressing gently but firmly on an idea until its structure, truth, and limitations emerge. Interrogation is not skepticism for the sake of being difficult. It is discipline for the sake of being accurate.

When you interrogate an idea, you are not looking for flaws — you are looking for shape. You ask what drives it, what assumptions it rests on, what trade-offs it implies, what pattern it belongs to, and what principle governs it. You examine whether the explanation is a mechanism or a metaphor, whether the claim is a cause or simply a coincidence. You search for the part of the idea that is stable and the part that is situational. This is how thinkers separate the essential from the decorative, the structural from the superficial.

Interrogation does not slow you down; it prevents you from running in the wrong direction. It keeps you from acting on incomplete assumptions, accepting convenient explanations, or mistaking confidence for correctness. The more you practice interrogating ideas, the more quickly you can identify their real value — whether they deserve adoption, adaptation, or dismissal. Leaders who interrogate ideas think with a level of clarity that others trust instinctively, not because they are louder or more certain, but because their thinking has been tested. They do not cling to answers; they refine them. They do not defend assumptions; they examine them. Interrogation is how ideas mature — and how thinkers do too.

Interrogation also protects your thinking from cognitive bias — especially the quiet pull of confirmation bias. When you question an idea instead of accepting the first explanation that feels comfortable, you prevent your mind from mistaking familiarity for truth.

51

The Reflection

Think about the last idea you accepted without questioning — perhaps a claim in a meeting, a suggestion from a colleague, or a belief you've held for years. What assumptions sat underneath it? What mechanisms supported it? What evidence contradicted it? Now think of a time when you *did* question an idea — when you pressed on it, explored it, or challenged it. How did your understanding change? Did the idea strengthen, weaken, or transform into something clearer?

Reflect on how interrogating ideas might change your work this week. Which decisions would benefit from clearer assumptions? Which explanations feel satisfying but untested? Which patterns deserve a second look? Interrogation is not about doubting everything — it is about ensuring that your thinking rests on stability rather than convenience. Consider what might open up for you if you made questioning a daily discipline instead of an occasional reaction.

Today shifts the work from processing ideas to challenging them, strengthening the architecture behind your understanding.

The Commitment

- I will question my first interpretation instead of accepting it as complete.
- I will test the assumptions beneath my explanations.
- I will practice slowing the urge to confirm what I already believe..

EBR Principle

Strong thinkers don't accept ideas — they test them.

Day 17 — Connecting New Concepts to What You Know (Practice Day #4)

The Lesson

Understanding accelerates when the mind has a way to anchor new ideas to existing structures. This is the essence of connection — the discipline of linking unfamiliar concepts to patterns, principles, and experiences already stored in your thinking architecture. Most people treat new ideas as isolated pieces of information. But abstract thinkers treat them as extensions of something they already understand. When a new concept arrives, they immediately begin searching for its neighbors: what it resembles, what it contradicts, what it strengthens, and what it reshapes.

Connection is not about forcing ideas into the wrong category. It is about discovering the right category — the one where the idea naturally fits and gains meaning. When you connect a new idea to something familiar, it becomes easier to remember, easier to work with, and easier to explain. Today's exercises will help you practice this bridging process: identifying the structure beneath a new idea, finding its closest conceptual relatives, and integrating it into your existing scaffolding. Once an idea has a place to belong, your mind can use it rather than simply store it.

Exercise 1 — Category Assignment Drill

List five concepts you've heard this week — terms, insights, instructions, or observations.

Sort each into one of your buckets:

- **Principle, Mechanism, Pattern, Behavior, Context**

Notice which ideas become instantly clearer once categorized.

Exercise 2 — Schema Mapping

Select a topic you find confusing. Draw a simple map:

- What you already know
- What you are unsure about

- What the new idea adds
- Draw lines showing how the pieces connect.

If you can visualize the relationships, you're building schema.

Exercise 4 — The Principle Finder

Choose any real-world problem or decision. Ask:

- *What principle governs this?*
- *What rule repeats across similar situations?*

State the principle in **one clean sentence**.

The Reflection

Which exercise revealed the most about the way your mind organizes information? Did bridging help you see a new idea more clearly? Did categorization simplify something that previously felt tangled? Did mapping expose gaps in your understanding you hadn't noticed? Many people discover during this practice that their confusion was never about the idea itself — it was about lacking the right connections to hold it in place.

Reflect on how often you treat new information as something separate rather than something that fits into an existing structure. As you move into the second half of the book, connection will become one of your most important tools. It turns learning into integration and information into capability. The stronger your connections, the faster your understanding grows. This practice stabilizes new understanding by linking unfamiliar ideas to the architecture you have already built.

The Commitment

- I will map new concepts onto structures I recognize.
- I will look for the mechanism beneath novelty.
- I will reinforce learning by connecting ideas instead of collecting them..

EBR Principle

New ideas become clear when they connect to old ones.

Day 18 — Standing in Unfinished Understanding

The Lesson

Every complex idea goes through an awkward middle stage — a period where you understand enough to see its potential, but not enough to articulate it cleanly. Most people retreat from this stage because it feels disorienting. They want full clarity immediately, and when it doesn't arrive, they assume they aren't smart enough or the concept is too difficult. But unfinished understanding is not a sign of failure. It is a normal — and necessary — part of abstract thinking. If you cannot stand in that space, you cannot grow beyond what you already know.

Standing in unfinished understanding means resisting the urge to collapse the idea prematurely. It means allowing ambiguity, contradiction, and partial clarity to coexist without forcing a conclusion. The mind needs time to build structure — to find the mechanism, identify the pattern, extract the principle, and connect the concept to what you already know. When you rush this process, you end up with a shallow interpretation or a convenient metaphor that won't hold up when tested. When you allow the process to unfold, the idea becomes more accurate, more stable, and more useful.

This discipline becomes even more important as ideas grow more abstract. Deep concepts rarely "click" in a single moment. They reveal themselves in layers, each one requiring a bit more patience and a bit more cognitive strength. The ability to stand in unfinished understanding is what separates those who master complex thinking from those who avoid it. It is the mental version of staying in the pocket under pressure — calm, focused, trusting the process rather than panicking at the unknown. You don't need to understand everything at once. You need to stay present long enough for the structure to form.

The Reflection

Think of a time when you abandoned a complex idea too early — not because it lacked value, but because it lived in that uncomfortable middle stage where comprehension felt out of reach. What might have changed if you had stayed with it just a little longer? Now consider a concept you *did* allow yourself to wrestle with. Perhaps it took days, weeks, or even years to fully understand. What did you learn about yourself during that process? Did the final clarity justify the discomfort that came before it?

Reflect on what happens internally when you encounter something you don't yet understand. Do you rush to simplify? Do you disengage? Do you assume you're not capable? Or do you give your mind the space it needs to build structure? Over the next few days, notice each moment you enter that middle stage. Instead of retreating, stay with the idea. Let the uncertainty be part of the work. Every deep thinker lives in this space more often than they admit.

This day teaches the discipline of holding meaning open long enough for patterns to form without forcing a conclusion.

The Commitment

- I will tolerate the discomfort of incomplete clarity.
- I will let meaning emerge instead of rushing to simplify.
- I will resist the urge to close a thought before it's ready..

EBR Principle

Clarity takes time. Stay in the work long enough for it to form.

Day 19 — Learning the Thing You Don't Yet Know

<u>The Lesson</u>

Most people assume that learning something new is difficult because the content is unfamiliar or because confusion is inherently uncomfortable. But abstract thinkers know this isn't true. Learning becomes difficult only when you lack the tools to organize the new idea. When you do have a reliable thinking system — buckets, scaffolding, compression, mechanisms, and principles — unfamiliar concepts stop feeling threatening. The mind is no longer entering unknown territory without support. It's entering unknown territory with a map, a compass, and a framework that can absorb whatever it encounters.

The real confidence in learning comes from trusting the system you've built. You know how to slow the input. You know how to sort ideas. You know how to compress the core. You know how to interrogate assumptions. And you know how to rebuild meaning in your own words. These tools give you a place to stand, no matter how new or complex the idea may be. The concept may be unfamiliar, but the process is familiar — and that changes everything. The mind relaxes. Curiosity turns on. Integration becomes easier because you already know the sequence for making sense of things.

Once you realize that learning something new is not chaos but a structured process, the unknown stops feeling like a threat. It becomes an invitation — a chance to apply your tools to a fresh idea. This is where the system pays dividends. It transforms novelty from something that destabilizes you into something that strengthens you. The idea doesn't need to be easy. Your process makes it workable. And the more you trust the process, the faster and more confidently you can absorb concepts that once felt out of reach.

The Reflection

Think back to a time when learning something new felt overwhelming. Was the difficulty in the concept itself, or in the absence of a method for making sense of it? Now consider a more recent moment — perhaps during this book — when you encountered something unfamiliar but felt more capable than before. Did your tools help you slow down, sort, compress, or connect the idea? How did that shift your confidence?

Reflect on how different learning feels when you trust your process. Instead of wondering whether you're capable, you begin asking, Which tool applies here? Which bucket should this go in? What's the mechanism underneath this? The system becomes your stability. Over the next few days, notice how often your confidence rises not because the idea is simple, but because your method is strong. That is the true power of a structured mind.

This work extends your capacity to think clearly in areas where your knowledge is limited or developing.

The Commitment

- I will work through unfamiliar concepts using structure rather than certainty.
- I will break complex ideas into components I can navigate.
- I will approach new domains with curiosity rather than avoidance..

EBR Principle

New ideas feel easier when your system is strong.

Day 20 — The Layers of Meaning

The Lesson

Every idea contains layers — surface statements, structural truths, underlying drivers, and governing principles. Most people stop at the surface. They interpret words literally, react to events immediately, and take explanations at face value. But abstract thinkers understand that the meaning of an idea is rarely found in the part that's easiest to see. It emerges from the layers beneath it: from the mechanism driving the behavior, from the pattern repeating across situations, and from the principle that gives the idea its stability. To understand something fully, you must learn to move through its layers rather than settling for the first one that presents itself.

This layering is not an academic exercise; it is essential to clarity. When you can separate surface signals from structural meaning, you stop being misled by noise. You stop confusing symptoms with causes, emotions with incentives, or explanations with mechanisms. Each layer gives you a different kind of insight: the surface tells you what happened, the mechanism tells you how it works, the pattern tells you what repeats, and the principle tells you why it must happen that way unless something changes. When you learn to navigate these layers intentionally, your understanding becomes deeper and your decisions become more accurate. "Layered thinking also shields you from attribution bias — the habit of blaming people for what systems, incentives, or constraints actually caused. When you move past the surface, you stop assuming intention where structure was really driving the outcome.

Working through layers of meaning requires patience, but it also requires confidence in your system. The tools you've built — buckets, scaffolding, compression, interrogation, systems thinking — allow you to move through the layers without getting lost. You know where to look for structure. You know how to reduce noise. You know how to ask the right questions. The idea doesn't have to be simple for you to understand it; it only has to be layered. And when you can see those layers clearly, you gain a level of insight that others mistake for intuition, but is actually the reward of disciplined thinking.

The Reflection

Think of a recent conversation, conflict, or decision that felt confusing on the surface. What layer were you interpreting it from at the time? Were you reacting to the visible signal, or did you consider the mechanism driving it? Did you notice any patterns that would have revealed deeper meaning? Now imagine revisiting that situation with the layers explicitly in mind: surface → mechanism → pattern → principle. How differently might you understand it now?

Reflect on how often you treat meaning as something that should appear immediately, when in reality, meaning is something you uncover by moving downward through structure. What layers do you tend to skip? Do you stop too early? Do you stay too long at the surface? Over the next few days, practice looking for the layers when new ideas arrive. Ask yourself: *What is the surface telling me? What is the structure beneath it? What repeats? What principle governs this?* The more consistently you apply this lens, the more clarity you will create not just in your thinking, but in your leadership.

This is the first of several days that examine different layers of understanding; each day explores a separate dimension of meaning. Here you begin to see that meaning operates in layers, each revealing a different dimension of what you observe.

The Commitment

- I will separate surface meaning from deeper mechanism.
- I will examine context, incentives, and structure before drawing conclusions.
- I will look beyond what is said to understand what is driving it.

EBR Principle

Meaning deepens as you move downward through the layers.

Day 21 — Week 3 Practice Lab (Practice Day #6)

The Lesson

This week expanded your thinking architecture in powerful ways. You learned how the mind accelerates with practice, how interrogation reveals the structure beneath an idea, how new concepts become clearer when linked to existing scaffolding, and how meaning emerges through layers rather than at the surface. These aren't abstract theories — they are tools meant to be used. Today's practice session helps you integrate them. Each exercise is designed to deepen your ability to work across levels of meaning, connect unfamiliar ideas to familiar structures, and move from surface to mechanism to pattern to principle with confidence.

This is the moment when your system begins to pay visible dividends. The more you use your tools, the more natural they become — and the faster clarity forms. Today's work is not about trying harder; it's about trusting the structure you've built. Treat each exercise as reinforcement training for a mind that can navigate complexity with precision.

Exercise 1 — The Layer Drill
Choose any recent event, idea, or conversation. Identify:
1. **Surface:** What happened
2. **Mechanism:** What drove it
3. **Pattern:** What repeats
4. **Principle:** What governs it

    One idea, four layers, one clearer understanding.

Exercise 2 — The Connection Builder
Select a new concept you encountered this week. Write:
- What existing idea it resembles
- How it strengthens or challenges your current scaffolding
- Which bucket it belongs in

This anchors the new to the known.

Exercise 3 — The Interrogation Pass

Pick an idea you think you understand.

Ask:

- *What assumption is this resting on?*
- *What evidence supports it?*
- *What mechanism actually explains it?*

    Write a brief clarification after the interrogation.

The Reflection

Reflect on how differently you think now compared to Day 1. Much of the acceleration you experience doesn't come from knowing more — it comes from *processing differently*.

Now consider how these tools are beginning to interact. When you connect a new concept, layering becomes easier. When you interrogate an idea, acceleration increases. When you trust your scaffolding, unfamiliar ideas feel more accessible. This is how systems of thinking grow — each discipline strengthens the others. Over the next week, notice how often your clarity comes not from the idea itself, but from the structure you've built to interpret it.

The Commitment

- I will practice identifying multiple layers within a single moment of understanding.
- I will shift between surface, mechanism, pattern, and principle deliberately.
- I will slow my thinking enough to see which layer I am reacting from.

EBR Principle

Clarity compounds when your tools work together.

Day 22 — Seeing Invisible Forces

The Lesson

Most people explain situations by looking only at what is visible: what someone said, what happened, what changed, what failed, or what succeeded. But abstract thinkers learn to look past the surface and identify the invisible forces shaping those outcomes. These forces include incentives, assumptions, constraints, mental models, system dynamics, cultural norms, and the unspoken rules that drive behavior. They are rarely obvious in the moment, yet they exert more influence than the visible event itself. When you can see these hidden layers, you understand not just what happened, but why it had to happen that way.

Invisible forces operate like gravity: you can't see them directly, but you can see their effects everywhere. A person's behavior is shaped by incentives more than intentions. A team's culture is shaped by norms more than policies. A system's performance is shaped by constraints more than effort. When you learn to identify these forces, you gain a level of insight that feels predictive. You stop being surprised by human behavior. You stop misreading problems as personal when they're actually structural. You stop reacting to symptoms and start addressing the deeper forces underneath them.

Seeing invisible forces does not require special intuition. It requires disciplined observation and an understanding of where to look. You ask what the system rewards. You examine what the system punishes. You consider what people fear, what they misunderstand, what they lack, and what pressures sit on them. You notice patterns across situations and connect them to the forces that repeat. As you build this skill, you become someone who sees reality with greater accuracy. You begin predicting outcomes not because you are guessing, but because you understand the forces driving the situation. This ability transforms how you lead, how you interpret behavior, and how you solve problems.

The Reflection

Think of a recent situation that confused or frustrated you. What invisible forces might have been shaping it? Consider incentives, constraints, fears, habits, or unspoken rules. How might the situation appear differently if you looked beneath the surface event and examined the pressures behind it? Now recall a moment when you *did* correctly read the forces at play — when you recognized what was really motivating someone or what limitation was truly driving an outcome. How did that recognition shift your response?

Reflect on how often misunderstandings in your world come from interpreting visible behavior without considering invisible forces. Ask yourself: *What force made this outcome predictable? What system made this behavior reasonable? What pressure made this reaction inevitable?* As you continue through the final stretch of the book, train your attention to look beyond what is said or done. The truth is almost always one layer deeper.

This is a narrower form of layering: instead of surface meaning, you are identifying structural forces that operate beneath visible behavior. Today reveals the structural forces that shape behavior beneath visibility, expanding your understanding of cause and effect.

The Commitment

- I will look for the incentives, constraints, and pressures that operate beneath visible behavior.
- I will distinguish intent from structure.
- I will notice when a force, not a person, is driving the outcome..

EBR Principle

What you can't see often explains what you can.

Day 23 — Thinking in Layers

The Lesson

Thinking in layers is the natural extension of everything you've built so far: buckets, scaffolding, compression, mechanisms, systems, patterns, and principles. Each of these tools lets you move up or down through different depths of meaning, seeing more than what's immediately visible. Layered thinking means you never treat an idea, behavior, or situation as a single-point event. You see the surface, yes — but you also see the structure beneath it, the forces around it, the history behind it, the incentives shaping it, and the principle governing it. When you think in layers, you gain dimensionality. You understand not just *what is happening,* but *the terrain it sits on.* Because layered thinkers never treat the first layer as the whole story, they naturally avoid oversimplification biases — the mental shortcuts that make quick explanations feel accurate even when they're incomplete.

Most people think on one layer at a time. They see a behavior without seeing the incentive, a decision without seeing the trade-offs, a conflict without seeing the underlying pattern, or a result without seeing the system that produced it. Layered thinkers zoom in and out fluidly. They shift from detail to structure, from structure to mechanism, from mechanism to principle, and back again — without losing their place. This flexibility allows them to make sense of complex situations quickly. They aren't overwhelmed by the layers because they know the order in which to navigate them.

Thinking in layers also prevents the costly mistake of overreacting to the surface. When you understand the deeper architecture, you respond with precision rather than emotion. You know which layer the real problem belongs to and which layers are merely noise. You can see when a situation is driven by misunderstanding rather than malice, by incentive rather than intention, by system rather than individual. This is what gives layered thinkers their steadiness. They don't jump at shadows because they know how to see the whole landscape. Layer by layer, situation by situation, they interpret reality with more accuracy than those who only look at the topsoil.

65

The Reflection

Think back to a situation that frustrated you this week — a conversation, a decision, or a moment where something didn't make sense. Which layer were you thinking on at the time? Were you stuck at the surface, reacting to what was said or done? Or did you look at the incentives, the constraints, the history, the forces, or the pattern underneath? Now imagine re-evaluating that same situation with layered thinking. How would the meaning change? What would suddenly make sense that didn't before?

Reflect on your natural tendencies: do you stay too long in the details? Do you jump too quickly to principles? Do you forget to check the system around the event? Over the next few days, notice which layers you move through automatically and which layers you tend to skip. The goal is not to be perfect at every layer but to navigate them deliberately — to choose the right depth rather than defaulting to the nearest one.

This day completes the layering progression by showing how the surface, mechanism, pattern, and principle interact inside a single moment of understanding. This day completes the layering progression by teaching you to navigate meaning across layers intentionally and in real time.

The Commitment

- I will practice switching layers as understanding deepens.
- I will widen or narrow my view to match what the moment requires.
- I will think across layers instead of reacting within one..

EBR Principle

Shallow thinking sees the moment. Layered thinking sees the meaning.

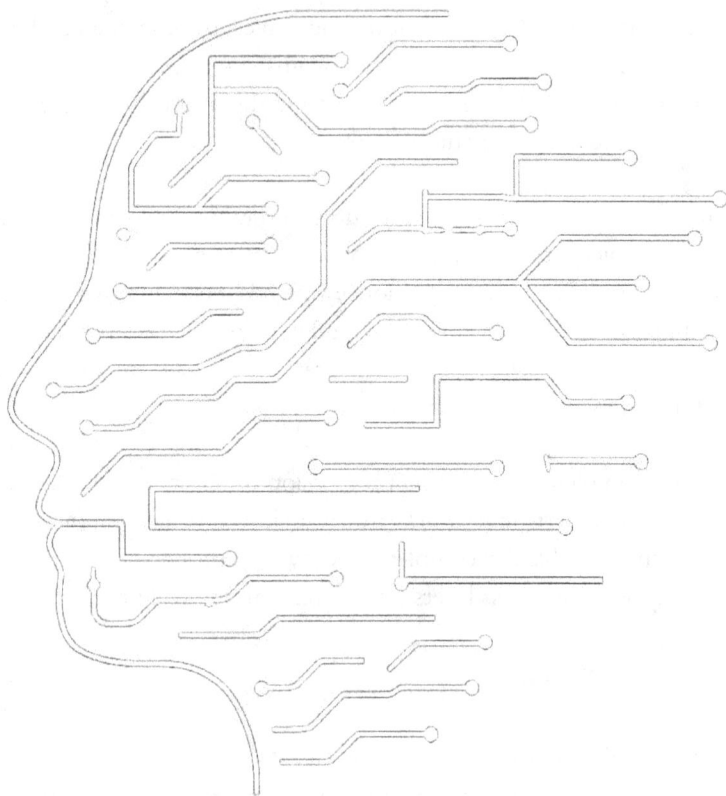

Transition For Days 24–30

The final days of this book shift from personal clarity to shared clarity. Up to this point, the work has focused on how you build understanding within your own mind: slowing information, structuring ideas, identifying mechanisms, and working across layers of meaning. Now the focus expands.

Days 24–30 move from internal architecture to external application. They show how clarity becomes action, how structured thought becomes leadership, and how understanding becomes something others can rely on. These days are not a departure from the earlier work; they are the natural extension of it. Once you can think with structure, the next step is to use that structure to stabilize the environment around you.

This final movement brings the system together. You will translate meaning, simplify without distortion, recognize principles in motion, and operate as someone who provides clarity where others experience complexity. This is the culmination of the thirty-day progression: thinking that not only understands, but also strengthens.

Day 24 — Turning Ideas Into Action

The Lesson

Clear thinking is valuable, but it becomes powerful only when it leads to action. Many people assume that understanding and execution are separate skills — one intellectual, one practical. But in reality, execution is simply the outward expression of well-organized thought. When your ideas are structured, compressed, categorized, and connected to principles, the path forward becomes obvious. The reason people struggle to act is not because they lack discipline, but because their thinking has not been shaped in a way that reveals what needs to happen next. Action is what emerges when clarity has been built correctly.

Turning ideas into action requires you to translate abstraction into movement. You must take something conceptual — a mechanism, a pattern, a principle — and determine how it manifests in a real situation. This translation is not guesswork. It follows a logic: understand the mechanism, identify the leverage point, determine the sequence, and choose the simplest step that honors the structure you've discovered. When the thinking is deep and accurate, the actions become precise and efficient. You stop taking random steps and start taking strategic ones.

The confidence to act does not come from certainty. It comes from the reliability of your process. When you know how to interrogate assumptions, when you understand the forces shaping a situation, when you can see the layers of meaning and the system around them, action becomes almost inevitable. You are no longer trying to "be decisive"; the structure of the idea pushes you forward. This is why abstract thinkers often appear calm in complex situations — they are not guessing. They are following the architecture. When your thinking is well-built, your actions inherit that stability. You act not because you are fearless, but because the next step is clear.

The Reflection

Think of a moment when you struggled to take action — perhaps on a project, a decision, or a conversation you kept postponing. Was the hesitation emotional, or was the thinking underneath it unclear? Now recall a moment when action came easily. What was different? Did you understand the mechanism behind the situation? Did you see the pattern? Did you identify the principle or the leverage point? These are the conditions that make action feel natural instead of forced.

Reflect on how often you blame yourself for "not acting" when the real issue is insufficient clarity. What would happen if you treated hesitation not as a failure of willpower but as a signal that the thinking needs to go one layer deeper? Over the next few days, notice how often the right action becomes visible the moment you organize the idea correctly. Structure creates movement. Organized ideas move you forward by design.

The Commitment

- I will translate understanding into movement.
- I will let structure guide my actions, not pressure or emotion.
- I will seek the leverage point rather than scatter my effort.
- I will treat clarity as the source of effective action.

EBR Principle

When the thinking is clear, the next step reveals itself.

Day 25 — Strategic Thought

The Lesson

Strategic thinking is often misunderstood as long-range planning or big-picture imagination. In reality, strategy is simply the disciplined ability to understand how actions compound over time. It requires you to think several layers deeper than the moment, to see the forces shaping the landscape, and to anticipate how today's choices echo into tomorrow's outcomes. Strategic thinkers do not guess the future — they understand the structure of the present so clearly that the future becomes easier to predict. They see the mechanism behind the system, the incentives behind behavior, the constraints that shape outcomes, and the patterns that repeat across time.

The foundation of strategic thought is abstraction. You cannot think strategically if you cannot compress information, identify principles, interrogate assumptions, or see problems in layers rather than fragments. Strategy emerges when you can step out of the immediate details and ask: *What is this really about? What is driving this? What will this become if nothing changes?* When you operate with that level of clarity, you stop reacting to events and start influencing trajectories. Strategy is less about choosing a destination and more about understanding the path that leads there.

What makes strategic thinking so powerful is that it is not dependent on certainty. You don't need perfect information to see direction. You need structure. When your mind is trained to map systems, identify leverage points, and recognize predictable patterns, you can see how a situation is likely to unfold. This doesn't mean you are locked into a rigid plan. It means you are guided by principles that make your thinking adaptable, stable, and resilient. Strategic thinkers don't bet on luck. They bet on structure. And because of that, their decisions accumulate over time — each one reinforcing the next, each one compounding into long-term impact.

The Reflection

Think of a situation in your life or work that requires long-term thinking. How have you been approaching it — as a series of isolated decisions, or as a system unfolding across time? Now consider what shifts when you apply the tools you've built: mechanisms, patterns, principles, layers, incentives, constraints, and systems. How does the situation look when viewed not as a moment but as a trajectory?

Reflect on whether your hesitation comes from uncertainty or from a lack of structure. True strategic clarity rarely comes from knowing everything — it comes from understanding the forces well enough to see direction even when details are missing. Over the next few days, practice identifying the "future echo" of your choices. What does this action set in motion? What pattern will it reinforce? What principle does it align with or violate? Strategic thinking is not mystical. It is the natural outcome of organized thought.

The Commitment

- I will view situations in trajectories, not moments.
- I will use mechanisms and principles to anticipate outcomes.
- I will let structure, not urgency, guide long-term decisions.
- I will think in layers to understand how actions compound.

EBR Principle

Strategy is clarity stretched across time.

Day 26 — Pattern Recognition

The Lesson

Most of what feels unpredictable in life is actually structured. Situations repeat. Behaviors repeat. Problems repeat. Systems repeat. When you learn to recognize these repetitions early — before they fully reveal themselves — thinking becomes significantly easier. Pattern recognition is not about seeing coincidences; it is about identifying meaningful structures that appear across different contexts, decisions, and personalities. The patterns are always there. The question is whether you have trained your mind to notice them.

Patterns emerge when your thinking is organized enough to see past the surface details. People who struggle with complexity often believe every situation is unique, forcing them to start from zero each time. But abstract thinkers know that uniqueness is mostly cosmetic. Beneath the noise, the same incentives drive behavior, the same mechanisms produce outcomes, and the same principles govern why events unfold the way they do. When you can spot these patterns, you reduce cognitive load instantly. You no longer need to build a new understanding from scratch; you simply identify the recurring structure and work from there.

Pattern recognition also strengthens your ability to anticipate outcomes. The moment you identify a familiar structure, you know which behaviors will follow, which failures are likely, which incentives will dominate, and which levers will matter most. This is not guesswork — it is applied structure. Once your mind begins to see patterns rather than isolated moments, you gain access to a kind of cognitive efficiency that accelerates everything else: decision-making, problem-solving, judgment, and leadership. Pattern recognition does not replace deeper analysis; it *primes* it. It gives you the first doorway into meaning, revealing where to look and what matters most.

The Reflection

Think of a situation this week that felt chaotic or surprising. Now ask yourself: *Have I seen this before?* What behaviors, incentives, or system dynamics repeated themselves? What made the situation feel new when the underlying pattern was actually familiar? Now consider the last time you recognized a pattern early — perhaps in someone's communication style, a project's failure mode, or the way a team responded to pressure. How did that recognition change your confidence or your decisions?

Reflect on the patterns you encounter most often: recurring conflicts, predictable bottlenecks, repeated misunderstandings, or familiar performance swings. What principle connects them? What mechanism produces them? What system sustains them? Awareness of patterns is not about predicting everything — it's about recognizing that most complexity is structured and therefore knowable. Over the next few days, notice how often the "new" is simply the "familiar" wearing different details.

The Commitment

- I will look for repeating structures beneath changing details.
- I will let patterns guide where I focus my attention.
- I will treat predictability as a function of structure, not intuition.
- I will use patterns to accelerate insight and reduce cognitive friction.

EBR Principle

Patterns make complexity predictable.

Day 27 — Thinking Without the Shortcut Traps

The Lesson

Human thinking runs on shortcuts. Your brain is designed to conserve energy, move quickly, and make meaning with as little effort as possible. These shortcuts — often called cognitive biases — aren't signs of weakness or gullibility. They're the default operating system of an unstructured mind. The danger is not that these shortcuts exist; the danger is when you rely on them instead of on the tools you've been building. Biases fill the gaps when structure is missing. But when your thinking is organized, categorized, scaffolded, interrogated, and layered, those shortcuts stop running the show.

Most biases arise from the same source: the brain's tendency to trust the first explanation that feels familiar. Confirmation bias, attribution bias, anchoring bias, pattern-imposition bias, and overconfidence bias all function by collapsing complexity into something quick and comfortable. But abstract thinkers replace comfort with structure. You don't need the shortcut when you have the system. When you interrogate ideas, you disrupt confirmation bias. When you move through layers, you disrupt attribution bias. When you compress ideas to their essence, you disrupt anchoring. When you connect new concepts to existing scaffolding, you disrupt misfitting patterns. Your tools do the work bias normally does — but with accuracy instead of distortion.

The goal is not to eliminate bias; it's to outgrow it. Bias thrives in the absence of discipline. It weakens under structure. It disappears when you apply buckets, mechanisms, patterns, and principles. As your thinking strengthens, the mind no longer reaches for shortcuts because it no longer needs them. You have a framework capable of processing complexity without collapsing it. You see ideas clearly without rushing toward the first available meaning. You're not fighting bias — you're replacing it with a system that makes thinking stable, deliberate, and reliable. This is what it means to think without the shortcut traps.

The Reflection

Where have shortcuts shown up in your thinking this week? Did you interpret someone's behavior too quickly? Did you trust the first explanation because it felt familiar? Did you overlook a structural cause because the surface meaning was more comfortable? Now think of a moment when you applied your tools — interrogation, layering, patterns, mechanisms — and felt bias weaken. What changed in your clarity? What changed in your confidence?

Reflect on which shortcuts you tend to default to: assuming intention, seeking quick certainty, trusting your first instinct, or misreading patterns into noise. These aren't flaws; they're invitations. Each bias reveals a place where structure wants to be strengthened. Over the next few days, notice when your mind reaches for speed. Slow down. Apply your tools. Let structure replace assumption. When your system is strong, shortcuts become unnecessary.

The Commitment

- I will replace mental shortcuts with structure.
- I will let interrogation interrupt my first assumptions.
- I will use layers and patterns to correct distortions.
- I will treat bias as a signal to apply better thinking, not as a flaw.

EBR Principle

Structure outperforms shortcuts.

Day 28 — Building Cognitive Models

The Lesson

A cognitive model is a mental blueprint — a structured representation of how something works. It is the architecture you build in your mind that allows you to understand, explain, and predict ideas without needing to relearn them every time. People who struggle with complexity often approach each new situation as if it is an entirely new event. But skilled thinkers build models. They create internal structures that capture the mechanism, the variables, the patterns, and the governing principles. Once a model exists, every new piece of information has a place to land. New ideas don't float around in isolation; they snap into the structure like a puzzle piece finding its home.

Cognitive models are not memorized diagrams — they are living tools. They grow as you refine understanding and shrink when you eliminate irrelevant detail. They represent the highest level of abstraction: the ability to compress complexity into a shape you can carry with you. When you have a model, you don't rely on instinct or raw memory. You reason from structure. You can test assumptions, anticipate outcomes, and reconstruct ideas from first principles because you know how the system behaves. Models transform scattered information into comprehension, and comprehension into capability.

The power of cognitive models is not just that they help you understand your world — it's that they help you teach it. When you can articulate how something works in a simple, stable structure, you make the invisible visible to others. You become someone who engineers clarity. This is why the best thinkers and leaders are model-builders. They don't just react to complexity; they organize it. They don't just solve problems; they explain them. A cognitive model becomes both a map and a multiplier: it guides your reasoning and it amplifies your ability to help others reason as well.

The Reflection

Think about a concept in your life or work that once felt overwhelmingly complex but slowly began to make sense over time. What model did you build, consciously or not, that allowed the pieces to fit together? What were the key mechanisms? What were the patterns? What principle unified the whole? Now consider an area where you currently lack a model — something that feels scattered, ambiguous, or frustrating. What would a model for that domain need to contain? What shape would it take? Which elements are structural and which are noise?

Reflect on the possibility that your discomfort with certain topics may come not from difficulty, but from the absence of a model. Over the next few days, start paying attention to the models you already rely on — for conversations, decisions, leadership, conflict, systems, learning, or judgment. You are further along than you realize. Once you can see your models clearly, you can strengthen them, refine them, and build new ones deliberately. This is how abstract thinkers turn insight into something stable, repeatable, and teachable.

The Commitment

- I will build models that make complexity understandable.
- I will use structure to replace confusion, not shortcuts.
- I will refine my models as I deepen my understanding.
- I will teach ideas through the models that clarify them.

EBR Principle

A model turns complexity into something you can carry.

Day 29 — Elegant Simplicity

The Lesson

As your thinking becomes stronger, a new challenge emerges: simplifying ideas without stripping them of their meaning. Many people confuse simplicity with reduction. They cut away so much that the idea collapses into something catchy but inaccurate. Elegant simplicity is different. It is the ability to compress complexity into a clear form while preserving the structure, the mechanism, and the principle that make the idea true. This skill is the hallmark of mature abstract thinking. It signals that you no longer rely on the surface; you understand the architecture well enough to rebuild it in fewer words.

True simplicity is earned. It comes only after you've moved through the layers, interrogated the assumptions, identified the forces, recognized the patterns, and built a cognitive model. Without that work, any attempt to simplify becomes flattening rather than clarifying. But with that work, simplicity becomes a service — a way to make meaning useful to yourself and accessible to others. The goal of elegant simplicity is not to make the idea smaller; it is to make the idea portable. A principle you can carry is more valuable than a concept you cannot lift.

Elegant simplicity also sharpens your judgment. When you can reduce a complex situation to its essential structure, you gain the ability to make decisions faster and with greater precision. You no longer sort through endless details or chase decorative explanations. You see the mechanism quickly, name the principle clearly, and act from a place of confidence rooted in understanding. The more you practice elegant simplicity, the more trustworthy your thinking becomes — not because it is brief, but because it is structurally accurate. Simplicity becomes not a shortcut, but a sign of mastery.

The Reflection

Think of a concept that once felt overwhelming but that you now understand well. If you had to express its essence in one or two sentences — without losing accuracy — what would you say? Notice how much of that clarity comes not from clever phrasing but from the structure you've built underneath the idea. Now consider an area where your explanations still feel tangled or too long. What's missing? A mechanism? A principle? A clear boundary? Elegant simplicity reveals where structure is strong and where it needs more work.

Reflect on the situations in your life where elegant simplicity could reduce confusion — in conversations, in leadership, in decisions, in teaching others. What could become easier if you consistently expressed ideas at their true level of clarity rather than at the level of detail? Over the next day, practice compressing one complex idea into its essential form. Let structure guide what stays and what goes.

The Commitment

- I will simplify with accuracy, not shortcuts
- I will preserve structure when compressing ideas
- I will use simplicity as proof of understanding
- I will make meaning portable for myself and others

EBR Principle

Simplicity is clarity after the work is done.

Day 30 — The Person Who Understands

The Lesson

Understanding is not a moment. It is a capability. By now, you have built something far more substantial than a set of techniques — you have built a thinking system. You have learned to sort ideas into buckets, build scaffolding, compress concepts to their essence, interrogate assumptions, recognize patterns, interpret layers, map systems, see invisible forces, and translate complexity into movement. These skills are not isolated; they form an architecture. And that architecture changes who you are. You are no longer someone who hopes for clarity. You are someone who generates it.

This shift is profound. Most people move through the world reacting to complexity, overwhelmed by the volume of information and the speed of events. But you now operate differently. You understand how ideas fit together. You know where to look when something doesn't make sense. You know how to move through confusion without collapsing into shortcuts or bias. You know how to build models that make the unfamiliar familiar. You see patterns others overlook. You can translate ideas into meaning and meaning into action. This is what it means to become the person who understands — not because you know everything, but because you can learn anything.

The person who understands moves through life with a quiet confidence. They don't pretend to be certain; they trust their process. They don't fear new ideas; they have a place to put them. They don't get lost in details; they know how to find the structure. They don't chase perfect knowledge; they build working clarity. Understanding becomes less about storing information and more about shaping it. And the more you use this system, the more natural it becomes. Thought becomes cleaner. Decisions become easier. Judgments become sharper. This is the beginning, not the conclusion, of a new way of thinking.

The Reflection

Look back at the way you approached complex ideas thirty days ago. How did you react to uncertainty? How did you handle ambiguity? How often did you settle for the first explanation that felt comfortable? Now compare that version of yourself to the thinker you are today. What tools changed the most for you? Which disciplines became second nature? Which layers of meaning do you now see automatically? Consider how much of this growth came not from effort, but from structure — from having a system that supports clarity instead of relying on willpower or intuition.

Reflect on what it might look like to carry this discipline forward. What will it change in how you lead, analyze, communicate, and decide? How might your relationships shift as your clarity deepens? How might your work improve as your thinking strengthens? You have built a system you can trust — one that will continue to sharpen and expand as you use it. Understanding is no longer something you hope for. It is something you practice. Something you create. Something you own.

The Commitment

- I will continue building the architecture of my mind
- I will apply the tools until they become instinct
- I will pursue clarity with structure, not shortcuts
- I will live as a person who understands

EBR Principle

Understanding is a discipline — and now, it is yours.

Bonus Day — The Art of Translation

The Lesson

Understanding is powerful, but translation is what makes it useful. To translate an abstract idea is to take something internal, layered, and complex and express it in a way that another mind can absorb. Translation is not simplification; it is precision. It is the disciplined ability to carry the mechanism, the structure, and the principle across the boundary between minds. When you translate well, you do more than communicate — you create understanding in someone else. And that is one of the rarest and most valuable capabilities a thinker can possess.

Most people speak from their conclusions. They offer answers without structure, opinions without mechanism, or instructions without meaning. Translated thinking works the opposite way. It begins by identifying the essential structure of the idea and choosing the clearest path to express it. You decide what layer matters, what mechanism drives the point, what pattern reinforces it, and what principle holds it together. You shape the idea so that it lands with coherence instead of confusion. Translation is a generosity: you do the cognitive work so the listener doesn't have to.

What makes translation so important is that it is the natural extension of understanding. When you truly understand something, you can rebuild it at any level — from the deep mechanism to the simple principle to the practical action. Translation proves comprehension. It also elevates your leadership, because people follow those who help them see clearly. Clarity reduces friction, strengthens trust, and accelerates alignment. The person who understands can move through the world with confidence; the person who understands *and can translate* can lift the understanding of everyone around them. That is the work of thinkers, teachers, and leaders — and now it is your work too.

The Reflection

Think of a moment when someone explained something to you so clearly that the idea clicked instantly. What made their translation effective? Did they isolate the mechanism? Reduce noise? Choose the right level of abstraction? Now consider a time when you tried to express a complex idea and felt it land unevenly. What was missing — structure, clarity, or the right frame? Translation is not about being articulate; it is about carrying the architecture of an idea across the bridge intact.

Reflect on the conversations, decisions, and relationships in your life that would benefit from stronger translation. Where would clearer thinking expressed clearly make work smoother, conflict lighter, or collaboration easier? Over the next week, choose one idea each day and practice translating it into its essential form. Do the structural work first. Then express it simply enough to be understood and strong enough to be true. This is the discipline that turns private understanding into shared clarity.

The Commitment

- I will translate ideas with structure, not shortcuts
- I will express meaning in its clearest and most accurate form
- I will carry understanding across the bridge between minds
- I will treat translation as the final expression of mastery

EBR Principle

When you understand deeply, you can make others understand.

What Changes After Day 30

After the program, three shifts typically occur:

1. You recognize structure faster — and noise more immediately.

Mechanisms, patterns, and layers begin to appear without effort. This is the acceleration effect.

2. Your mind returns to old habits under pressure.

Speed, assumption, and urgency can override structure if you don't maintain the architecture.

3. Your thinking becomes more teachable.

The clearer your internal models become, the more you naturally express clarity to others. Your thinking becomes stabilizing.

The extension plan is designed to strengthen these three shifts and prevent regression.

How to Prevent Regression

Regression does not happen suddenly. It happens subtly through:

• letting pace override structure
• skipping buckets and scaffolding
• operating at the surface layer
• failing to interrogate assumptions
• allowing emotions or incentives to distort interpretation

The antidote is predictable: **small, consistent engagement with the architecture.**
Not intensity — rhythm.

Monthly Thinking Calibration Drills

Conduct these once every 30 days.
They keep the system tuned.

Drill 1 — Reconstruct an Idea From Scratch

Choose a complex idea and rebuild it using mechanism, pattern, principle, and compression.
This strengthens reconstruction and accuracy.

Drill 2 — Map a System You've Been Operating Inside

Identify flows, constraints, loops, and leverage points.
This sharpens system recognition.

Drill 3 — Translate an Abstract Concept for Someone Else

Use structure, not story.
Translation is the capstone skill — the final proof you understand.

Drill 4 — Perform a Pattern Scan

Look across a week, a project, or a relationship.
What repeats? What governs it?
Pattern clarity increases foresight.

Drill 5 — Build or Refine One Cognitive Model

Pick a domain (decision-making, communication, leadership, quality, strategy).
Refine your model so it becomes more compressed, more accurate, and more reusable.

These drills take 30–40 minutes each but compound into transformative clarity over a year.

Weekly Thought-Architecture Audit

Perform a five-question review at the end of each week:

1. **Where did I lose structure?**
   Identify the moment pace, emotion, or assumption distorted clarity.
2. **Where did I rely on the surface instead of the mechanism?**
   Name at least one example.
3. **Where did I successfully use the tools?**
   Reinforce the wins. Skill grows through recognition.
4. **What pattern did I notice this week?**
   Patterns reveal direction and reduce cognitive load.
5. **What is one idea I should compress and record?**
   Compression strengthens recall, alignment, and portability.

A weekly audit prevents drift and keeps clarity conscious until it becomes instinct.

How to Expand Your Models Over Time

Your cognitive models should not remain static. They mature the same way expertise matures — through contact with real conditions.
Expand your models by focusing on four evolving dimensions:

1. Breadth (Where the model applies)

Apply the model in new contexts. If it holds, the model strengthens; if it breaks, refine the mechanism.

2. Depth (How many layers the model can support)

Add nuance: invisible forces, deeper incentives, secondary mechanisms. Depth increases accuracy.

3. Compression (How cleanly the model can be expressed)

Every model should move toward a one-sentence governing principle.

4. Transferability (How easily the model teaches)

A model is not complete until someone else can use it.

Expansion transforms a personal framework into an expert-level mental tool.

The Goal of the Extension

The purpose of the next 30 days is not to repeat the program, but to:

• reinforce the architecture
• strengthen the structural habits
• prevent regression
• extend your models
• integrate the tools into your real-world environment

The system becomes permanent when structure becomes your default response to complexity.
This extension is how that permanence is built.

The 10 Mistakes That Break Clarity (And How to Avoid Them)

Clarity is not lost all at once. It erodes through predictable mistakes that narrow attention, distort meaning, or accelerate interpretation before structure is complete. These mistakes appear in every domain where information moves quickly and the consequences of being wrong matter. Recognizing them allows you to correct course before the loss of clarity becomes a loss of alignment or decision quality.

1. Rushing to understand before slowing the input

Clarity collapses when pace overrides precision.
Avoid it: Begin by slowing information enough for structure to form.

2. Treating every detail as equally important

This creates noise instead of meaning.
Avoid it: Sort information into buckets before interpreting it.

3. Explaining events with narrative instead of mechanism

Stories feel intuitive but hide causality.
Avoid it: Identify what is causing what.

4. Closing meaning before all layers are visible

Premature conclusions distort interpretation.
Avoid it: Hold unfinished understanding long enough for patterns to emerge.

5. Treating assumptions as facts

Assumptions accelerate thinking but weaken accuracy.
Avoid it: Label what is known, unknown, and assumed.

6. Overcomplicating the problem

Adding detail feels productive but obscures structure.
Avoid it: Compress the idea without losing its shape.

7. Confusing intent with behavior

This misattributes cause and leads to inaccurate explanations.
Avoid it: Look for incentives and structures that make an outcome likely.

8. Ignoring the mechanism of the system

Symptoms dominate when structure is overlooked.
Avoid it: Examine the flow, dependencies, constraints, and cycles beneath events.

9. Talking before thinking

Communication without structure spreads confusion rather than clarity.
Avoid it: Translate understanding into a stable form before expressing it.

10. Attempting to think in isolation

Ideas stabilize when exposed to other perspectives.
Avoid it: Check alignment by asking others to restate the idea.

These mistakes are common because they are easy. Avoiding them is uncommon because it requires structure, patience, and awareness. With practice, each becomes a signal that clarity is forming—or slipping—and a reminder to return to the architecture you've built across these thirty days.

The Real Conditions of Thought

Clear thinking does not occur in controlled or pristine environments. It unfolds inside real conditions—pressure, uncertainty, time constraints, incomplete information, and the natural reactions of the human mind. Structure stabilizes these conditions, but it does not eliminate them. Understanding how thought behaves under pressure allows you to recognize what is shaping your interpretation before it shapes your decisions.

Thought is influenced by internal forces long before you notice them. Urgency pushes the mind toward fast explanations that feel decisive even when structure is incomplete. Ego seeks confirmation and protection, favoring interpretations that reinforce prior beliefs or preserve position. Assumption fills gaps quickly, often without evidence. Ambiguity discomfort leads to premature closure, turning a developing insight into a fixed conclusion before the pattern has fully formed. Familiarity encourages the mind to rely on previous experiences even when the current mechanism is different. Emotional momentum carries over from one moment to the next, quietly reshaping what you notice and how you interpret it.

External conditions interact with these internal forces. High-velocity environments reward speed in ways that quietly penalize accuracy. Teams that rely on rapid alignment reinforce first interpretations. Organizational habits—unquestioned routines, unwritten rules, and inherited narratives—create default explanations that feel true simply because they are shared. The mind drifts toward these patterns because they reduce cognitive effort, not because they increase understanding.

These forces do not signal flawed reasoning. They signal natural cognitive responses to uncertainty. The problem arises when they operate unnoticed. When urgency overrides mechanism, when ego narrows interpretation, when assumption substitutes for evidence, the mind treats reactions as understanding. Clarity becomes distorted not by a lack of intelligence, but by a lack of awareness of the conditions in which thinking is taking place.

Structured thinking provides a counterweight. Slowing input interrupts urgency. Sorting information exposes assumption. Identifying mechanism prevents narrative from replacing structure. Working across layers separates surface meaning from deeper drivers. Compression forces precision. Translation ensures that meaning does not distort as it moves between people. Together, these practices reduce the influence of internal interference by giving thought an ordered path to follow.

The real conditions of thought will always include friction, uncertainty, and the pressure to decide before understanding is complete. The purpose of the system you have built is not to create a frictionless environment, but to help you navigate one. When you recognize the forces shaping your thinking, you create space for clarity to emerge. When you apply structure consistently, understanding stabilizes even when the conditions do not.

The work of thinking is never separate from the environment in which it occurs. It becomes reliable not when conditions improve, but when structure becomes strong enough to guide you through them.

Applied Examples — A 30-Day Reference Guide

How to Use This Section

This section provides a practical companion to the thirty daily lessons. Each example illustrates how the ideas in the book appear in real situations: meetings, decisions, investigations, conversations, and moments of interpretation. The goal is not to add new content, but to give you a clear anchor for seeing the concepts in motion.

Use these examples in three ways:
• To reinforce understanding after completing each day
• To check your ability to recognize the structure of thinking in real scenarios
• To revisit the entire system after the 30 days and observe how the patterns connect

The examples are brief on purpose. They are not case studies or stories. They are demonstrations of how abstract thinking takes shape when applied with structure, clarity, and intention.

Treat this section as a reference guide you can return to any time you need to clarify a concept, test your comprehension, or strengthen the architecture you've built over the past thirty days.

Day 1 — Thinking Is a Skill, Not a Trait

A supervisor believed he "just wasn't analytical," especially during problem-solving meetings. After slowing conversations down and asking mechanism-based questions, he began spotting causal links others missed. Nothing about the equipment changed; only the structure of his thinking did. Once he treated thinking as a trainable skill, clarity increased and his confidence followed.

Day 2 — Slowing Input to Increase Understanding

A manager misinterpreted a rapid sequence of updates in a production meeting and left believing three unrelated issues were connected. When he reviewed the notes slowly afterward, the actual driver was a single constraint in the flow path. The information was the same, but slowing the input allowed meaning to form accurately.

Day 3 — Conceptual Buckets

A team debated whether a recurring delay was a communication issue, a behavior issue, or a system issue. Once they bucketed it as a *mechanism* problem, the conversation shifted: the delay always appeared when a specific dependency lacked clarity. The issue hadn't been vague — it had simply been placed in the wrong category.

Day 4 — Mental Scaffolding

An engineer faced a complex vendor report that felt overwhelming until she drew a simple scaffold showing Inputs → Process → Output. With that frame in place, irrelevant details fell away and the core mechanism became visible. The clarity didn't come from knowing more; it came from giving the information a structure to sit inside.

Day 5 — Cognitive Compression

A lengthy email thread described frustration about missed deadlines, competing priorities, and unclear roles. When compressed, the entire situation reduced to one sentence: "Decisions are being made after work begins instead of before." Compression transformed scattered detail into organized meaning.

Day 6 — Tolerating Ambiguity

A leadership team wanted an immediate explanation for a sudden drop in performance. One analyst resisted the rush to certainty and held the ambiguity long enough to observe that the drop occurred only after a specific upstream change. The insight emerged not from speed, but from tolerating the discomfort of an unfinished idea.

Day 7 — Practice Lab #1

A planner examined a confusing set of maintenance notes that appeared inconsistent. Once he sorted observations into buckets — pattern, mechanism, detail, and behavior — a structure emerged. The issue repeated only after a common setup step. Organization revealed what quick reading could not.

Day 8 — How the Mind Sorts Information

A team entered a meeting with twenty competing data points. When they sorted the details by type — constraint, noise, requirement, and signal — only two inputs actually drove the outcome. The moment the information was categorized, the decision became straightforward.

Day 9 — Mechanism Over Metaphor

Operators referred to a recurring stoppage as "temperamental equipment," a metaphor that sounded plausible but offered no leverage. Once someone examined the mechanism, they discovered a thermal cutoff activating under specific load conditions. The mechanism replaced the narrative, and the problem became solvable.

Day 10 — Cause → Pattern → Principle

A supervisor noticed one operator repeatedly bypassed a minor alarm. Reviewing past weeks showed the same behavior across multiple people during similar conditions. The principle became clear: people will prioritize throughput when the system rewards speed over procedure. The moment the principle surfaced, the corrective action shifted from coaching to system redesign.

Day 11 — Thinking in Systems

A bottleneck appeared to originate at a single workstation, but mapping the system revealed a feedback loop between scheduling, staffing, and equipment readiness. The workstation wasn't the cause; it was the output of the system's structure. Seeing the system allowed the team to address the leverage point instead of the symptom.

Day 12 — Working Memory Strength

A manager struggled to hold multiple competing priorities during a meeting. After establishing buckets for decisions, constraints, and questions, his mental load decreased and he could reason more clearly. His capacity hadn't changed — only the organization of the information had.

Day 13 — Reconstruction Over Recall

A trainee could repeat a new procedure's steps but became confused when asked to explain why each step mattered. When she reconstructed the process in her own words, she began understanding the underlying mechanism. Recall produced familiarity; reconstruction produced mastery.

Day 14 — Practice Lab #2

A technician listed five failures that seemed unrelated. After extracting patterns, he noticed each failure occurred immediately after a similar adjustment made under time pressure. Identifying the pattern allowed the team to address the true driver rather than treating them as isolated issues.

Day 15 — The Acceleration Effect

At first, a new supervisor needed considerable time to sort information and build structure before making decisions. After several weeks of consistent categorization and compression, he began spotting patterns almost instantly. Speed appeared not because he rushed, but because his internal architecture strengthened.

Day 16 — Interrogating Ideas

A team assumed their new process was failing due to operator resistance. Once they interrogated the idea, they uncovered an untested assumption: operators didn't understand the sequence because the documentation was written from a design perspective rather than a user perspective. Challenging the assumption exposed the real cause.

Day 17 — Connecting New Concepts to What You Know

A leader learned a new communication model and initially found it abstract. When she mapped it to mechanisms and patterns already familiar from continuous-improvement work, the new idea became far easier to apply. Connection turned novelty into clarity.

Day 18 — Standing in Unfinished Understanding

A manager examined recurring turnover data that didn't yet make sense. Instead of forcing a conclusion, he allowed the partial picture to remain unfinished while more information arrived. Over time, a multi-layered pattern surfaced that would have been missed had he insisted on immediate clarity.

Day 19 — Learning the Thing You Don't Yet Know

An engineer received a technical report in an unfamiliar domain. Using sorting, compression, and mechanism-first questions, she broke the concept into workable components. The report didn't become easier — her method made it manageable.

Day 20 — The Layers of Meaning

A conflict between two departments looked interpersonal on the surface. Examining deeper layers revealed a structural mechanism: one team depended on upstream information that routinely arrived late, creating predictable tension. Once the mechanism and pattern were identified, the principle governing the conflict became clear.

Day 21 — Practice Lab #3

A project manager revisited a stalled initiative. Layering the situation revealed: surface (missed deadlines), mechanism (unclear inputs), pattern (late decisions), and principle (flow precedes execution). With the layers aligned, the next step became obvious.

Day 22 — Seeing Invisible Forces

A supervisor couldn't understand why a team resisted a new procedure despite training. Looking deeper, he found an invisible force: following the procedure increased cycle time, which lowered their performance rating. When the incentive changed, the behavior changed immediately.

Day 23 — Thinking in Layers

A meeting escalated over a misunderstanding of responsibilities. At the surface, it appeared personal. At the structural layer, roles were ambiguous. At the incentive layer, the teams were rewarded differently. Seeing the layers reframed the situation from conflict to misalignment.

Day 24 — Turning Ideas Into Action

A leader understood a system problem conceptually but struggled to act. Once she identified the mechanism and the single leverage point, the next step became clear: restructure the information flow, not the personnel. Action followed naturally once structure clarified direction.

Day 25 — Strategic Thought

A manager evaluated whether to invest in new equipment. Instead of treating it as a one-time decision, he examined how the constraints, incentives, and demand patterns would evolve over time. Strategy emerged from understanding the system's trajectory rather than its moment.

Day 26 — Pattern Recognition

A recurring issue seemed unpredictable until someone compared five instances side by side. The same trigger appeared each time: a specific upstream variability. Recognizing the pattern allowed the team to anticipate the issue before it occurred.

Day 27 — Thinking Without the Shortcut Traps

A team initially assumed a delay was caused by poor communication because that explanation felt familiar. After interrogating assumptions and reviewing system structure, they discovered a sequencing flaw. The shortcut explanation was comfortable; the structured explanation was correct.

Day 28 — Building Cognitive Models

A quality engineer struggled with defect reports until she built a simple cognitive model of how variation propagated through the process. Once the model existed, new data points snapped into place automatically. The model turned complexity into something she could predict and teach.

Day 29 — Elegant Simplicity

A complicated discussion about capacity planning spiraled into details. When someone expressed the entire issue as "Demand variability exceeds the system's ability to absorb it," the room aligned instantly. True simplicity preserved the structure while removing the clutter.

Day 30 — The Person Who Understands

During a multi-department meeting, conflicting explanations surfaced. One participant listened, sorted the inputs, identified the mechanism, recognized the pattern, surfaced the principle, and expressed the clarity in one clean sentence. Understanding didn't make him louder — it made him stabilizing.

Cognitive Bias Countermeasures Tool

A practical guide for restoring clarity when thought becomes distorted by internal shortcuts.

Biases appear whenever the mind tries to resolve uncertainty too quickly. They reduce the search for understanding by narrowing attention, simplifying mechanisms, or closing meaning prematurely. These countermeasures do not eliminate bias; they redirect thinking back toward structure.

Use these patterns as signals and the practices as stabilizers.

1. **Confirmation Pressure**

   Distortion: The mind prefers information that supports the first interpretation.
   Countermeasure: Interrogate the idea (Day 16). Ask: *What would disprove this? What mechanism would contradict it?*
   This moves thought from protection to examination.

2. **Anchoring**

   Distortion: The first detail becomes the foundation for the entire explanation, even if irrelevant.
   Countermeasure: Slow the input (Day 2). Restate the situation without the first detail and rebuild meaning from structure rather than sequence.

3. **Narrative Pull**

   Distortion: The mind assembles a story faster than evidence supports.
   Countermeasure: Return to mechanism (Day 9). Describe only what is causing what. Remove interpretation until structure becomes clear.

4. Premature Closure

Distortion: The mind reaches a conclusion before patterns or layers have formed.
Countermeasure: Hold unfinished meaning (Day 18). List what remains unknown. Delay the conclusion until all layers align.

5. Familiarity Bias

Distortion: New situations are interpreted as if they mirror past events, even when mechanisms differ.
Countermeasure: Separate surface from mechanism (Day 20). Identify what is truly the same and what is merely similar.

6. Emotional Carryover

Distortion: Present emotion reshapes the interpretation of unrelated information.
Countermeasure: Compress the idea (Day 5). Reduce the situation to its mechanism in one sentence. Structure weakens emotional projection.

7. Assumption Drift

Distortion: Unstated assumptions begin acting as facts.
Countermeasure: Sort information (Day 8). Label each element as *known*, *unknown*, or *assumed*. Challenge each assumption directly.

8. Overconfidence

Distortion: Clarity is assumed rather than demonstrated.
Countermeasure: Check alignment through translation. Ask another person to restate the idea. If the structure changes, clarity was incomplete.

9. **Recency Distortion**

Distortion: Recent events overshadow the true pattern across time.
Countermeasure: Examine the pattern (Day 10). Extend the timeline. Identify whether the recent event reinforces or contradicts the larger structure.

10. **Intent Attribution**

Distortion: The mind assigns motive where only behavior or structure is observable.
Countermeasure: Look for invisible forces (Day 22). Replace the question "Why did they do that?" with "What incentive or structure made this outcome likely?"

How to Use This Tool

You do not need to identify each bias precisely.
You only need to notice when your thinking becomes tight, fast, or overly certain.

When that happens:

1. Recognize the pattern that resembles your contraction.
2. Apply the countermeasure drawn from the 30-day architecture.
3. Return to structure, not to the story.

This tool is not about avoiding bias;
it is about **re-stabilizing clarity whenever internal forces distort interpretation.**

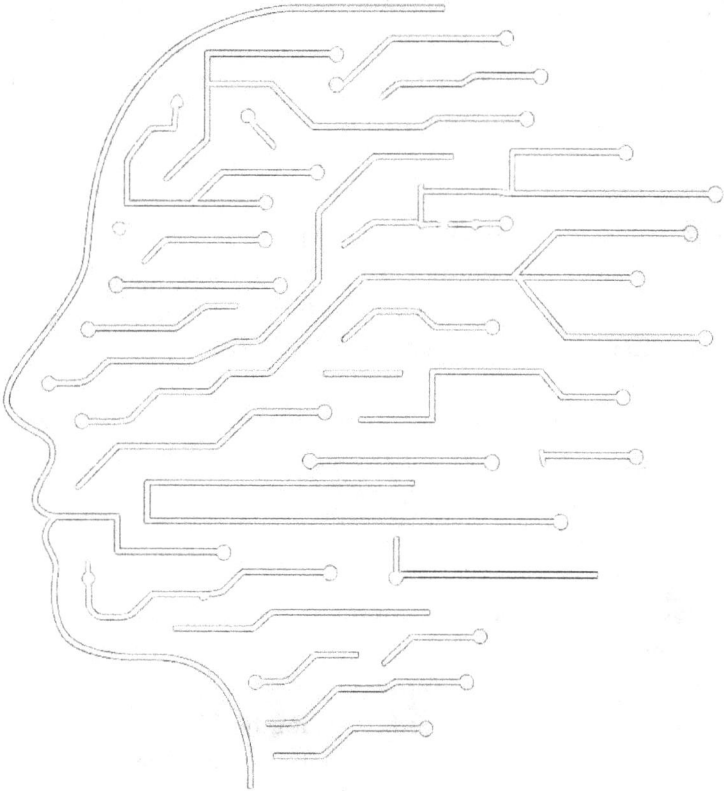

Full System Example

How to Use This Full-System Example

By the end of the thirty days, you will have practiced each individual skill of abstract thinking: slowing input, sorting information, identifying mechanisms, recognizing patterns, layering meaning, compressing ideas, and translating understanding into action. Each skill matters on its own, but their full value appears when they operate together.

The following example demonstrates the entire architecture as a single, integrated process. It shows how a complex situation becomes navigable when examined through the structure you have built across the month. This is not a case study to memorize. It is a demonstration of what it looks like when the tools align into a coherent method of thinking.

Use this example to reinforce the progression of ideas, strengthen your mental model of the system, and clarify how each element contributes to stable understanding and confident action.

A Practical Demonstration: How the 30-Day Architecture Works Together

A multi-department project had stalled for the third time in six months. The symptoms looked familiar: missed deadlines, unclear decisions, repeated handoffs, and growing frustration. Each group had its own explanation, and none of them matched. Before any solutions were proposed, the situation was examined through the structure developed across the 30 days.

The information was slowed. Instead of treating all updates as equal, the inputs were sorted: constraints, requirements, assumptions, dependencies, and noise. With the information categorized, the mechanism became visible. The project was not failing because of behavior or effort. It was failing because decisions were being made after downstream work had begun, forcing constant rework.

Patterns connected past and present. Each previous stall had occurred under the same condition: upstream clarity was incomplete whenever timelines compressed. What appeared to be inconsistency was, in fact, a stable pattern driven by the same incentive and the same structural weakness.

Layers of meaning reinforced the diagnosis. The surface frustration was about missed targets. The deeper layer was misaligned information flow. Beneath that was the incentive structure: speed was rewarded more visibly than accuracy. At the base layer was the principle: systems produce outcomes that match their design, not their intent.

Compression turned a complex narrative into a single, usable sentence: **"The project fails whenever decisions lag behind execution."**

This clarity revealed the leverage point. The solution was not additional resources, new procedures, or more detailed planning templates. The solution was sequencing: decisions needed to be made before work began, not alongside it. Once that mechanism was stabilized, the project recovered quickly and consistently.

The full structure of abstract thinking was visible in the outcome.
Slowed input created comprehension.
Sorting created structure.
Mechanisms revealed causes.
Patterns created predictability.
Layers created depth.
Principles created alignment.
Compression created clarity.
And clarity made the action obvious.

This is the power of operating with a disciplined architecture for thought: complexity becomes navigable, decisions gain stability, and meaning becomes something you can build rather than chase.

The Abstract Thinking Operational Checklist

Use this checklist whenever you need to move from complexity to clarity. It is not a sequence to follow rigidly, but a set of stabilizing actions that anchor structured thought.

1. Slow the Input

- Pause long enough for information to separate into manageable pieces.
- Remove urgency from interpretation.

2. Sort the Information

- Identify what is signal, what is noise, and what is missing.
- Place each piece into a conceptual bucket.

3. Identify the Mechanism

- Ask: What is actually causing what?
- Separate metaphor from structure.

4. Examine the Pattern

- Look across time, conditions, or repetition.
- Determine whether the event is isolated or systemic.

5. Work Across Layers of Meaning

- Surface: What happened?
- Mechanism: Why did it happen?
- Pattern: When does it happen?
- Principle: What general rule is operating beneath it?

6. Compress the Idea

- Reduce complexity without losing structure.
- Express the core meaning in a stable, portable form.

7. Translate the Meaning

- Adjust the form for the audience while preserving the underlying structure.
- Aim for alignment, not agreement.

8. Decide the Leverage Point

- Identify the smallest action that changes the system meaningfully.
- Act from structure, not reaction.

9. Check for Human Interference

- Notice ego, urgency, assumption, or defensiveness.
- Reset the architecture if clarity slips.

10. Revisit and Adjust

- New information may require refinement.
- Stability comes from returning to structure, not from holding a fixed conclusion.

This checklist turns the 30-day architecture into a practical tool you can apply in any environment where clarity matters.

Re-Entry: How to Restart the System

Every reader will drift at some point—miss a day, lose momentum, or move too quickly through a lesson without absorbing it. This is normal. The architecture of thinking is not built through uninterrupted streaks; it is built through returning to structure whenever clarity begins to slip. Re-entry is part of the process, not a failure of it.

Restarting does not require beginning the book again. It requires re-establishing the conditions that make structured thinking possible. When the system feels distant or your understanding feels scattered, use the following sequence to regain orientation:

1. Slow the Input

Pause long enough for your mind to separate signal from noise. Rushing here repeats the pattern that caused drift.

2. Revisit the Core Tools

Return briefly to sorting, scaffolding, and compression—the elements that stabilize meaning. One page of review is enough to reset your architecture.

3. Reconnect With Mechanism

Identify the mechanism driving the situation in front of you, even if your understanding feels incomplete. Mechanism restores direction.

4. Choose a Starting Point

Select the next day you have not meaningfully completed, or the day where you lost clarity. Do not duplicate days unless the concepts feel genuinely unfinished.

5. Reduce the Scop

Treat the next day as a single practice cycle, not a return to the entire 30-day commitment. Small cycles rebuild momentum.

6. Reenter Without Judgment

Drift is part of cognitive work. What matters is your ability to return to structure, not your ability to maintain a perfect streak.

Re-entry is a skill in its own right. Each time you reengage with the architecture, you strengthen the habits that make clarity stable. The purpose of this guide is not to push you back into the system with force, but to remind you that the system is always available, and that understanding builds through returning, not through perfection.

About the Author

Andy E. Page, Jr., Ph.D.

Founder, **EBR Technologies**
Creator of the **Evidence-Based Reliability (EBR)™ and RCM-FX™**
frameworks

Andy Page is a reliability engineer, strategist, and educator who has spent more than two decades helping industrial organizations transform the way they think about maintenance, performance, and culture. His work bridges two worlds — the precision of data and the discipline of leadership.

As the founder of **EBR Technologies**, Andy developed the Evidence-Based Reliability (EBR) framework, a practical approach that helps teams replace emotion with evidence and chaos with control. His **RCM-FX** method redefines classical reliability-centered maintenance with deeper categorization of failure effects, layered protection logic, and a culture-first mindset that connects the shop floor to the boardroom.

Over his career, Andy has guided clients across manufacturing, utilities, energy, and consumer goods — helping leaders and technicians alike build systems that think before they break. His teaching style combines technical clarity with cultural insight, making reliability not just a technical function, but a leadership behavior.

When he's not writing or consulting, Andy speaks to global audiences about the intersection of foresight, data, and discipline — and how evidence can become the most trusted voice in an organization.

About EBR Technologies

EBR Technologies (Evidence-Based Reliability) is a reliability consulting and training organization focused on helping clients build systems that think, plan, and act with discipline.

Founded on the belief that reliability isn't assumed — it's engineered, EBR Technologies equips organizations with tools and frameworks to:

- Engineer foresight through structured analysis and evidence-driven planning.
- Strengthen execution through Work Execution Management (WEM) systems that eliminate friction.
- Shape culture through the R^3/R^4 Model — aligning what leaders Require, Reward, and Reinforce with what the organization's Rituals, Rhetoric, Role Models, and Routines display.

EBR's work spans reliability improvement roadmaps, criticality analysis, PM optimization, asset walkdowns, and full-scale cultural alignment programs designed to make evidence the language of leadership.

EBR Technologies
Evidence is our authority.

www.ebrtechnologies.com
info@ebrtechnologies.com

Author's Note on the Use of AI

This book was written in collaboration with an artificial intelligence tool — not as a shortcut, but as a companion in reflection.

Every lesson, mindset, and maxim within these pages originates from my years of teaching, consulting, and field experience in safety, reliability, and culture. The principles draw from my established models — the R3/R4 Culture Framework, the Evidence-Based Thinking philosophy, and the broader discipline of Leadership Alignment that I've practiced and refined across industries and organizations.

AI served here as an instrument, not an author. Like a disciplined editor with infinite patience, it helped shape language, surface clarity, and maintain consistency across hundreds of pages. But the thoughts, logic, and voice are entirely my own. Each reflection began with lived experience — moments in real plants, real teams, and real failures that taught what alignment truly means.

The machine assisted in structure; the meaning came from the field. It allowed me to capture ideas at the speed they occurred, to test phrasing against the very principles this book teaches — precision, coherence, and intent. The goal was never to let technology think for me, but to let it think with me, mirroring the process of inquiry that defines evidence-based leadership itself.

Every page has been reviewed, edited, and approved by me to ensure it aligns with the purpose of this work. The message is unchanged, whether typed by hand or accelerated by algorithm.

This book stands as proof that technology, when guided by experience and anchored by purpose, can amplify clarity without diluting conviction. The thinking remains human. The evidence remains real. The alignment remains intentional.

— *Andy Page Ph.D.*